The All-New
UNIVERSITY
CHALLENGE
Quiz Book

Compiled by
Steve Tribe

QUADRILLE

First published in 2015 by Quadrille

Foreword by Peter Gwyn
Text © *University Challenge*™ and ITV Ventures Limited 2015. *University Challenge*™ is produced in association with The College Bowl Company.

Quadrille is an imprint of Hardie Grant www.hardiegrant.com.au

Quadrille Publishing
Pentagon House
52–54 Southwark Street
London
SE1 1UN
www.quadrille.co.uk

ISBN 978 184949 7015

British Library Cataloguing-in-Publication Data. A catalogue record for this book is available from the British Library.

Publishing Director: Sarah Lavelle
Art Director: Helen Lewis
Designer and Editor: Steve Tribe
Cover Design: Two Associates and Gemma Hayden
Printed and bound by RODESA in Spain

10 9 8 7 6 5 4 3 2 1

Contents

Foreword

It's curious to think that what started out as a radio quiz programme in the USA in the 1950s should have become one of the most enduring fixtures of British television. Taken up by the fledgling Granada Television franchise, *University Challenge* first appeared on our screens in 1962 and very little has changed in over fifty years: it is no longer in black and white, of course; it has seen the presenter change from Bamber Gascoigne to Jeremy Paxman; and it has moved from ITV to BBC Two, but otherwise it is the same show it was when Harold Macmillan was Prime Minister, and most people had yet to hear of The Beatles.

The programme attracts around three million viewers a week, a figure that has remained steady for many years, in contrast to some of the bigger beasts of the television landscape who have seen their viewing figures eroded by the competing attractions of multi-channel broadcasting and the internet. Clearly, *University Challenge* viewers are steadfast, loyal, and less easily distracted.

But why has it remained so popular? It can't be the complexities of the format, because there aren't any in this programme with only one basic rule: answer a starter question correctly on your own, and your team will earn the chance to confer on three bonus questions. There's no more to it than that. It's hard, too, to attribute its popularity to the oldest, creakiest special effect in television, in which one team appears to sit on top of the other.

Perhaps a more likely reason is simply that there are plenty of people in Britain who value the benefits of a liberal education, and who enjoy the spectacle of young people embracing those values with often staggering displays of knowledge, both general and specific. Some of those young people go on to achieve an enduring public profile: Stephen Fry, Clive James, Miriam Margolyes, Sebastian Faulks, John Simpson and Julian Fellowes are among the programme's distinguished alumni. But for the majority it may be the only time they appear on television, described by a certain J. Paxman as 'a medium of incandescent superficiality'.

The questions in this book, therefore, pay tribute not only to the talented, resourceful and very clever team of writers and verifiers who produced them, but also to those very gallant teams of students who have attempted to answer them in full view of the public gaze.

For over five decades *University Challenge* has been cherished, debated and celebrated as a champion of excellence; it's been spoofed and parodied, made headlines, suffered accusations of elitism and gender imbalance, and used to justify any number of arguments about higher education. But, as Jeremy Paxman says to each student team when they enter the recording studio, bracing themselves for what might be a glorious win or an ignominious defeat: 'Have fun, just enjoy yourselves. Remember – *it's only a quiz.*'

Peter Gwyn
Executive Producer, *University Challenge*

Match One

1 Identify the poet who wrote these words:
'Oh, talk not to me of a name great in story;
The days of our youth are the days of our glory;
And the myrtle and ivy of sweet two-and-twenty
Are worth all your laurels, though ever so plenty.'

Three bonus questions on Holyroodhouse

a. The palace of Holyroodhouse in Edinburgh contains within its grounds the ruined abbey founded in 1128 by which king of Scotland? According to legend, it commemorates his miraculous survival of a hunting accident during the Feast of the Cross.

b. In 1687, Holyrood Abbey was adapted by King James the Seventh of Scotland to serve as a chapel for which order of chivalry?

c. Following the adaptation of the chapel, James the Seventh ordered the building of which church to serve as the parish church of Holyroodhouse? It is still used by the present monarch during her periods of residence in the city.

2 Quote: 'Human speech is like a cracked kettle on which we tap crude rhythms for bears to dance to, while we long to make music that will melt the stars.' Translated from the French, this statement appears in which novel of 1857, thought by contemporaries to have been offensive to public morals?

Three bonus questions on French dramatists

a. The seventeenth-century French dramatist and actor Jean-Baptiste Poquelin, described by Voltaire as 'the Painter of France', is better known by what stage name, adopted in about 1643?

b. Which of Molière's contemporaries, known for his tragedies, including *Andromaque* and *Phèdre*, also wrote one comedy, *Les Plaideurs*, a satire on the French legal system?

c. Which eleventh-century Spanish soldier and national hero was the subject of a tragedy by Pierre Corneille in 1637, which had huge popular success but sparked a literary controversy?

3 According to the curator of the Prado museum in Madrid in 2007, 'comin', meaning the spice cumin in a local dialect, was the family name of the painter usually known by what epithet, a reference to his father's profession of dyer?

Three bonuses on expressions whose two words are spanned by the name of a Greek letter; for example, the words 'tiresome game' contain the letter 'omega'. In each case, give the two-word expression and the Greek letter.

a. A Gloster Meteor, Boeing 747, McDonnell Douglas F-4 Phantom or an Airbus A-380?

b. Legislation of 1715 that authorised magistrates to command, upon pain of death, the dispersal of groups of twelve or more people who were 'tumultuously assembled'?

c. A length of 15.24 centimetres, expressed in imperial measurements?

4 Rayleigh-Taylor, Kelvin-Helmholtz and Rayleigh-Bénard
are all types of what general physical phenomenon,
characterised by the unbounded growth of small
disturbances?

Three bonus questions on politics in the nineteenth century

a. After a speech made there in 1834 by Sir Robert Peel,
which Staffordshire town gives its name to a 'manifesto'
that is often regarded as the foundation of modern
Conservatism?

b. In the manifesto, what act did Peel describe as 'a final
and irrevocable settlement, which no friend to peace
would attempt to disturb'?

c. 'The Tamworth Manifesto was an attempt to construct
a party without principles.' Who wrote these words in a
novel of 1844? He later succeeded in splitting the Liberal
Party to pass the Reform Act of 1867.

5 *The Choice of Hercules, Liberty in the Age of Terror* and
Against All Gods are works by which philosopher, a
regular columnist for *The Guardian* until 2013?

Three bonus questions on philosophy

a. Also used in mathematics and biochemistry, what term
is often used in logic for any inference whose premises
do not entail its conclusions?

b. Challenging the rational basis of any such inference,
which eighteenth-century Scottish philosopher's
argument is often credited with raising the problem of
induction in its modern form?

c. Which English philosopher advocated an eponymous
method of induction in the *Novum Organum* as a means
of studying and interpreting natural phenomena?

6 Meaning 'horizontal rope' in Japanese, what is the highest rank in Sumo wrestling?

Three bonus questions on a scientific term

a. Later superseded by 'electrons', what term did J.J. Thomson use to describe the negatively charged sub-atomic particles discovered during his study of cathode rays?

b. Meissner's corpuscles are encapsulated spring-like nerve endings situated near the surface of which organ of the body?

c. Speculating that elastic particles emitted by luminous bodies produce the sensation of vision when they fall on the eye, which British scientist published his corpuscular theory of light in 1704?

7 What initial three letters link: a city in North China that was destroyed by an earthquake in 1976, the lake in Ethiopia that is the source of the Blue Nile, and a seaport in Northern Morocco that gives its name to a small, sweet citrus fruit?

Three bonus questions on the novels of George Eliot

a. What was George Eliot's first full-length novel, published in 1859 and based, in part, on a story told to her by her aunt of a confession of child-murder she had heard in prison?

b. Given the epithet 'the Radical', who is the title character of Eliot's novel of 1866, set during the time of the Reform Act of 1832?

c. Set in the years before the 1832 Reform Act, which novel by Eliot features a brother and sister who grow up by a river near the village of St Oggs?

8 Originally thought to secrete nasal mucus but now seen to play a key role in endocrine regulation and the control of growth, development and metabolism, which small gland lies at the base of the brain in vertebrates?

> **Three bonus questions on pairs of words whose spelling differs by the substitution of a 'double-o' for a 'single-o' in the middle, for example 'cop' and 'coop'. In each case, give both words from the definitions provided.**
>
> **a.** 'The bouquet of wine or whisky' and 'a loop with a running knot, sometimes used to symbolise marriage'?
>
> **b.** 'Built with a hemispherical vault' and 'destined for catastrophe'?
>
> **c.** 'One with an unusual fondness for alcohol' and 'carbonaceous deposit in chimneys'?

9 In the Cartesian RGB system of colour, what would be seen if red, green and blue were of equal value and at their maxima?

> **Three bonus questions on a colour**
>
> **a.** The 'yellow spot', or *macula lutea*, is a feature of which organ of the body?
>
> **b.** What is the Chinese name of the Yellow River, so called because of the immense quantities of yellow silt it carries?
>
> **c.** Which hormone is produced by the *corpus luteum*, the spheroid of yellowish tissue that grows within the ruptured ovarian follicle after ovulation?

10 What single-digit number links: the element boron, the fourth root of 625, and the planet Jupiter's position from the Sun?

Three bonus questions on medicine

a. Now rarely used, which drug was developed in the 1940s and was the first antibiotic to be effective against tuberculosis?

b. The only vaccine now commonly available for protection against tuberculosis is named after its discoverers, and is usually known by what three initials?

c. The causative agent of TB in humans is *Mycobacterium tuberculosis*, infection by the related strain *Mycobacterium bovis* having been virtually eliminated in developed countries by what public health measure, first proposed in the 1880s?

11 What short name links: the highest station on the national rail network in England; the author of *Larpers and Shroomers* and *Fanboys and Overdogs*; and the protagonist of *The Hitchhiker's Guide to the Galaxy*?

Three bonus questions on science and mountains

a. Which mountain in central Italy gives its name to the large particle physics laboratory buried within it, which holds an experiment searching for dark matter?

b. Which peak in the Harz mountains in Germany gives its name to the phenomenon in which an elongated shadow of the observer, often bearing a halo, is cast on a layer of cloud?

c. On which mountain in California is the 100-inch Hooker telescope, used by Edwin Hubble to reveal the expansion of the universe?

12 Give the US city and state that is the location of the third-oldest of the Ivy League universities, founded in 1746?

Three bonus questions on the Solar System

a. Which planet has an equatorial diameter close to twice that of the Earth's moon?

b. Which planet has an equatorial diameter around one-tenth that of Neptune?

c. With a difference between equatorial and polar diameters almost as great as the actual diameter of Earth, which planet, by virtue of its size and rapid spin, has the largest equatorial bulge?

13 Following the example of the Cadbury brothers' model at Bourneville, which manufacturer and philanthropist developed the model village of New Earswick, north east of York?

Three bonus questions on unusual transportations

a. In which Booker Prize-winning novel by Peter Carey do the title characters become involved in a wager to transport a glass church into the Australian bush?

b. Which German director made the 1982 film *Fitzcarraldo*, in which the protagonist hauls a riverboat over a mountain in Peru in an attempt to finance the building of an opera house?

c. Based on a novel of 1950, Henri-Georges Clouzet's film *The Wages of Fear* concerns an attempt to transport what substance by jeep across dangerous terrain in South America?

14 Listen very carefully. Which word in this question contains the same number of letters as its immediate predecessor?

> **Three bonus questions on words that may be made from the letters of the word 'broccoli'. In each case, give the word from the definition.**
>
> **a.** An Italian word meaning 'liveliness', 'dash', 'vigour' or 'spirit'?
>
> **b.** A programming language created by Grace Hopper and others in 1959, and intended for use in commerce?
>
> **c.** An attack of severe spasmodic abdominal pain?

15 Give the chemical symbol that comes next in this sequence: B, C, N, O, F – and what?

> **Three bonus questions on probability distributions. In each case, give the name of the distribution being described.**
>
> **a.** The discrete distribution taking the value 1 with probability p, and taking the value 0 with probability 1 minus p?
>
> **b.** The discrete distribution that results from summing n independent Bernoulli random variables?
>
> **c.** The continuous distribution obtained as a limit of binomial distributions as n tends to infinity but p does not tend to 0?

16 Initially described as 'a solution looking for a problem' and, somewhat fancifully, as 'a death ray that is brighter than the Sun', the first successful version of what device was built by Theodore Maiman in Malibu in 1960? Its many uses include speed cameras, CD players, eye surgery, tattoo removal and barcode scanners.

Three bonus questions on astrophysical objects

a. What name is given to rapidly rotating neutron stars that emit regular beams of electromagnetic radiation, usually at radio frequencies?

b. What term indicates highly magnetised pulsars emitting mainly X-rays and gamma rays?

c. What term is used to describe highly redshifted active galactic nuclei surrounding a supermassive black hole?

17 Resembling a cornet but having a slightly larger bell, which instrument is a standard in British brass bands, its name being the German for 'wing horn'?

Three bonus questions on abbreviations

a. The economic theory that the true rate of exchange between two currencies can be determined by what can be bought with a unit of each is known as PPP; for what do these initials stand?

b. Founded in 1888, which US collegiate women's sorority has the initials DDD?

c. The radioactive element roentgenium, named after the German physicist, originally had a systematic element name referring to its atomic number 111, resulting in what three-letter symbol?

18 'Lenient ethics' is an anagram of the single-word name of which landlocked state, noted for its banking privacy policies and low rates of income tax?

Three bonus questions on chemical elements

a. The first three letters of which Group Two element form a word meaning 'unit of pressure'?

b. The first four letters of which Group Three element form a word meaning 'test the metre of a line of verse'?

c. The first five letters of which Group Seven element form a word that means 'Japanese-style comic books'?

19 The name of which British prime minister appears in historical expressions which also contain the words 'poodle' and 'declaration'? The former refers to the House of Lords, the latter to a letter of 1917 supporting the establishment of 'a national home for the Jewish people'.

Three bonus questions on a physicist

a. Which Welsh physicist gives his name to the phenomena that occur when an electric current passes through a very thin insulating layer between two superconducting substances?

b. Also named after Josephson, what devices are used in a large integrated circuit to speed the passage of signals by electron tunnelling?

c. The components of the Josephson Junctions only operate at temperatures close to what?

20 What is the common name of songbirds of the genus *motacilla*? British species include the yellow, grey and pied.

Three bonus questions on visual illusions

a. In 1900, the Polish-born US psychologist Joseph Jastrow introduced an ambiguous figure that can be seen as both a rabbit and which other animal?

b. In 1980, the English psychologist Peter Thompson illustrated the illusion of normality in a facial image, with eyes and mouth inverted relative to the face, using a photo of which public figure?

c. Which Austrian physicist gives his name to an illusion of 1866 consisting of an ambiguous line drawing of a folded sheet of paper?

21 Give either of the similar-sounding words that indicate the author of the seventeenth-century religious work *Grace Abounding* and a painful swelling on the big toe?

Three bonus questions on optometry

a. What condition of the eye is associated with elevated intra-ocular pressure as measured by tonometry?

b. If the grid of an Amsler chart appears distorted or has missing lines, what eye condition is indicated?

c. What refractive error is corrected by spectacles with concave lenses?

22 After a type of shell, what eight-letter noun denotes a plane curve consisting of two branches situated about a line to which they are asymptotic, so that any line through a fixed point intersecting both branches is of equal and constant length between asymptote and either branch?

Three bonus questions on a devil

a. What name for a demon, later sometimes applied to the Devil himself, was originally found in a German legend about a scholar who gives his soul to the Devil in exchange for unlimited knowledge?

b. Noted for his 1956 screen portrayal of Mephistopheles, the German actor Gustaf Gründgens was the inspiration for the novel *Mephisto* by which German author, who questioned his actions during the Nazi era?

c. Also based on the Faust legend, the *Mephisto Waltzes* were written between 1859 and 1885 by which Hungarian composer?

23 In 2010, which tennis player became the seventh player to win all four Grand Slam tournaments when he defeated Novak Djokovic in the US Open men's final?

Three bonus questions on a shared place name

a. Suffering extensive fire damage in the American Civil War during the occupation led by General Sherman, which city is the state capital of South Carolina?

b. The Canadian province of British Columbia is bordered by Alaska to the north west and by three other US states to the south. Washington is one; what are the other two?

c. The district of Columbia, with which the city of Washington is coextensive, lies on the bank of which river, forming the border between Maryland and West Virginia?

24 Some of the tallest sand dunes in the world are found in which coastal desert, lying between the Kalahari Desert and the Atlantic Ocean, and extending from Angola to St Helena Bay in South Africa?

Three bonus questions on theatre

a. 'Self-pitying snivel' is how the *Evening Standard* greeted the premiere in 1956 of which three-act play, whose action takes place in a one-room flat in the Midlands?

b. Which influential theatre critic and enthusiastic supporter of the play wrote in a much-quoted review, 'I doubt if I could love anyone who did not wish to see *Look Back in Anger*'?

c. Described by Tynan as 'the completest young pup in our literature since Hamlet, Prince of Denmark', which character is the protagonist of *Look Back in Anger*?

25 The UK Space Agency, launched in 2010, is based in which town to the west of London? The same town has featured in two James Bond films, was the home of the first lending library, has a group of five conglomerated mini-roundabouts known as the Magic Roundabout, and was home to a branch of Wernham Hogg in the sitcom *The Office*.

Three bonus questions on terminology

a. Popularised from the 1950s, what two-word term refers to the disorientation experienced by those who move from one environment or country to another that is markedly different?

b. Popularised by US historian Theodore Roszak in the title of a work of 1969, what term describes the lifestyle and approach of those who reject or oppose the dominant values of conventional society?

c. Which historian emphasised culture as the way groups 'handle' the raw material of social and material experience in his 1963 work *The Making of the English Working Class*?

26 Which art gallery links *How It Is* by Miroslaw Balka, *Shibboleth* by Doris Salcedo, *Embankment* by Rachel Whiteread, *Marsyas* by Anish Kapoor and *The Weather Project* by Olafur Eliasson?

Three bonus questions on a musical instrument

a. The dulzian, the sordone and the curtal are earlier versions of which double-reed instrument of the orchestra?

b. Using the highest notes of the instrument's range, a bassoon solo opens Stravinsky's score for which ballet, first performed in Paris in May 1913, with choreography by Nijinsky?

c. In Prokofiev's *Peter and the Wolf*, a bassoon plays the theme depicting which human character?

27 What is the three-letter stage name of the London-born musician of Sri Lankan descent, Mathangi Arulpragasam, who reached number four on America's Billboard 100 in 2008 with her single 'Paper Planes'?

Three bonus questions on human physiology

a. What common name is given to the substance found in the blood, brain and gastrointestinal tract which plays an important part in haemostasis and is involved in sleep, mood changes and prolactin secretion?

b. Which hormone is produced from serotonin and fluctuates in its concentration in the blood, being at its highest during darkness, and is thought to help to regulate circadian rhythms?

c. Which small gland in the brain synthesises melatonin and plays an important role in determining seasonal breeding patterns in some mammals?

28 Launched by Dennis Crowley and Naveen Selvadurai, which mobile phone application is a social networking service and geo-location game that, on 8 October 2010, awarded the UK's first 'super swarm' badge to 300 users who all checked into the Jewel bar in Piccadilly?

Three bonus questions on the films of David Lean. In each case, identify the film from its description.

a. Based on a novel by the French author Pierre Boulle, a 1957 Oscar-winning film starring Alec Guinness?

b. Based on a play by Noël Coward, a 1945 film starring Trevor Howard and Celia Johnson?

c. Based on a novel by Charles Dickens, a 1946 film starring John Mills and Valerie Hobson?

29 What is the only non-metric distance recognised by the governing body of international athletics, the IAAF, for world record purposes?

Three bonus questions on eponymous spacecraft

a. Which mission was launched in 1997 to explore Saturn and its natural satellites and was named after two seventeenth-century astronomers, one Italian and one Dutch, both of whom made major discoveries about the planet's moons and rings?

b. Thought to have been depicted by the painter Giotto in a fresco in Padua in the early fourteenth century, which celestial body was studied at close range for the first time by a probe named after the artist in March 1986?

c.	Which spacecraft mapped the surface of Venus from 1990 to 1994, and was named after a Portuguese explorer whose round-the-world voyage 470 years earlier had contributed to a similar understanding of the nature of the Earth?

30	'Chain', 'double treble', 'reverse half double' and 'slip stitch' are all terms used in which handicraft, whose name is a diminutive of the French word for 'hook'?

Three bonus questions on place names in County Durham. In each case, name the locality from the description.

a.	Which town shares its name with the family name of the earls of Derby and, hence, both the main town of the Falkland Islands and a North American ice hockey trophy?

b.	Which new town is named after a miners' leader who died in 1935?

c.	Which town has a name meaning 'Roman fort on the Roman road'?

The Answers

1️⃣ Byron ('Stanzas Written on the Road between Florence and Pisa, November 1821')
- **a.** David the First (Dabid mac Mail Choluim)
- **b.** The Order of the Thistle (The Most Ancient and the Most Noble Order of the Thistle)
- **c.** Canongate Kirk

2️⃣ *Madame Bovary* (by Gustave Flaubert)
- **a.** Molière
- **b.** (Jean-Baptiste) Racine
- **c.** *Le Cid / El Cid* (criticised by Richelieu's Académie Française for not obeying the unities)

3️⃣ Tintoretto (Italian *tintore*)
- **a.** Jet aircraft / jet aeroplanes, and *eta*
- **b.** The Riot Act, and *iota*
- **c.** Six inches, and *xi*

4️⃣ Instability
- **a.** Tamworth
- **b.** The Great Reform Act / the 1832 (Parliamentary) Reform Act
- **c.** (Benjamin) Disraeli

5️⃣ (Professor) A.C. Grayling / Anthony Grayling
- **a.** Induction
- **b.** (David) Hume
- **c.** (Francis) Bacon ('Baconian method')

6 Yokozuna (so called from the sacred straw rope presented to the Grand Champion)
  - **a.** Corpuscles
  - **b.** The skin / epidermis
  - **c.** Sir Isaac Newton

7 TAN (Tangshan, Tana, Tangier)
  - **a.** *Adam Bede* (Hetty Sorrel abandons her illegitimate child in a field, where it dies of exposure)
  - **b.** Felix Holt
  - **c.** *The Mill on the Floss* (Tom and Maggie Tulliver)

8 The pituitary gland (the literal meaning is 'snot gland')
  - **a.** Nose and noose
  - **b.** Domed and doomed
  - **c.** Sot and soot

9 White
  - **a.** The eye (accept retina, correcting it; the area lies slightly to the side of the centre of the retina that constitutes the region of best vision)
  - **b.** Huang Ho / Huang He (which also means Yellow River)
  - **c.** Progesterone

10 Five
  - **a.** Streptomycin
  - **b.** BCG (Bacille / Bacillus Calmette-Guérin)
  - **c.** Pasteurisation (of cow's milk)

11 Dent (in Cumbria, Susie and Arthur)
  - **a.** Gran Sasso (or Gran Sasso d'Italia)
  - **b.** The Brocken / Blocksberg / Bocksberg (the Brocken Spectre)
  - **c.** Mount Wilson / Wilson's Peak

12 Princeton, New Jersey
  - **a.** Mars

    b.   Mercury

    c.   Saturn

⑬ Joseph Rowntree (1836–1926; not to be confused with his son, Seebohm Rowntree)
- **a.** *Oscar and Lucinda*
- **b.** (Werner) Herzog
- **c.** Nitroglycerin

⑭ Contains
- **a.** Brio
- **b.** Cobol (Common Business Oriented Language)
- **c.** Colic

⑮ Ne (boron, carbon, nitrogen, oxygen, fluorine, neon; elements numbers 5–10)
- **a.** Bernoulli distribution (accept Bernoulli / Bern. [p])
- **b.** Binomial distribution (accept Binomial / Bin [n.p.] / B [n.p.])
- **c.** Normal distribution (accept Normal Gaussian distribution / Gaussian / Bell curve / Standard normal distribution)

⑯ LASER (Light Amplification by Stimulated Emission of Radiation)
- **a.** Pulsars
- **b.** Magnetars
- **c.** Quasars

⑰ Flugelhorn
- **a.** Purchasing Power Parity
- **b.** Delta Delta Delta / Tri-Delta
- **c.** UUU (unununium)

⑱ Liechtenstein
- **a.** Barium (bar)
- **b.** Scandium (scan)
- **c.** Manganese (manga)

19 (Arthur) Balfour (1848–1930)
    a. (Brian) Josephson (i.e. the Josephson Effect)
    b. Josephson Junctions
    c. Absolute zero (i.e. 0 K, -273.15 C, -459.6 F)

20 Wagtail
    a. Duck
    b. Margaret Thatcher
    c. Ernst Mach (the Mach Illusion)

21 Bunyan / bunion
    a. Glaucoma
    b. Macular degeneration / age-related macular degeneration / ARMD
    c. Myopia / short-sightedness / near-sightedness

22 Conchoid
    a. Mephistopheles
    b. Klaus Mann (if they answer just 'Mann', prompt for which one; Klaus was the son of Thomas; also at one time Gründgens' brother-in-law)
    c. Franz Liszt

23 Rafael Nadal
    a. Columbia (not Columbus, which is the state capital of Ohio)
    b. Idaho and Montana
    c. The Potomac (not Anacostia, a tributary of the Potomac that flows through Maryland and part of Washington but is not part of the West Virginia border)

24 Namib (Desert)
    a. *Look Back in Anger*
    b. Kenneth Tynan
    c. Jimmy Porter

25 Swindon (*The World Is Not Enough* and *A View to a Kill* both used Swindon as a filming location)
  a. Culture shock
  b. Counter-culture (*The Making of a Counter-Culture*)
  c. E.P. Thompson

26 Tate Modern (all have been exhibits in the Turbine Hall)
  a. Bassoon
  b. *The Rite of Spring / Le Sacre du Printemps*
  c. (Peter's) Grandfather

27 M.I.A.
  a. Serotonin (also known as 5-hydroxytryptamine)
  b. Melatonin
  c. Pineal (gland)

28 Foursquare
  a. *Bridge over the River Kwai*
  b. *Brief Encounter*
  c. *Great Expectations*

29 One mile / the mile
  a. Cassini-Huygens (Giovanni Domenico Cassini, Christiaan Huygens)
  b. Halley's comet
  c. (Ferdinand) Magellan

30 Crochet (not knitting or embroidery)
  a. Stanley
  b. Peterlee (Peter Lee, 1864–1935; Newton Aycliffe takes its name from a nearby village)
  c. Chester le Street (Chester, from the Anglo-Saxon for a Roman fort, Street for a Roman road)

Match Two

1. Named after a mathematician born in Sheffield in 1805, which physical theorem states that a charged particle cannot be held in a stable equilibrium by electrostatic forces alone?

Three bonus questions on emblems

a. Existing in several variants from 1922 to 1991, the state emblem of the Soviet Union showed a hammer and sickle superimposed on what?

b. The coat of arms of which EU member state includes a hammer and sickle, one quite separate from the other, in the two talons of an eagle?

c. A winged hammer and sickle is the logo of which Russian corporation, formerly a state-run enterprise of the USSR?

2. In an urn containing five balls, all of different colours, how many different combinations of colours are possible if you draw out three?

Three bonus questions on sorrow in Shakespeare. In each case, identify the play in which the following lines appear.

a. 'When sorrows come, they come not single spies, but in battalions'?

b. 'Let's talk of graves, and worms, and epitaphs; / Make dust our paper, and with rainy eyes / Write sorrow on the bosom of the earth'?

c. 'Parting is such sweet sorrow / That I shall say good-night till it be morrow'?

(3) What is the common name of the garden weed *Equisetum arvense*? It reproduces by means of spores and has invasive, deep-rooted rhizomes which make it difficult to control.

Three bonus questions on a royal office

a. Which royal office was created with the appointment of Nicholas Lanier in 1626 during the reign of Charles the First?

b. In 2004, the tenure of the Master of the Queen's Music was reduced from life to ten years to give more composers the opportunity to take up the position; who was appointed to the role in that year?

c. In 1985, the Master of the Queen's Music, Malcolm Williamson, composed Songs for a Royal Baby in honour of whose birth?

(4) Reputed to be the noisiest amphibian in Europe, *Epidalea calamita* has what common name? The smallest and rarest of our two native British toads, it is characterised by a thin, bold, yellow dorsal stripe and a tendency to run rather than hop.

Three bonus questions on astronomy

a. To the nearest ten million, what is the mean distance in kilometres from the Earth to the Sun, that is, one astronomical unit?

b. To the nearest ten, how many astronomical units is the mean distance from the Sun to the outermost undisputed planet, Neptune?

c. Now more than 110 astronomical units from Earth, what was the first manmade object to leave the Solar System?

5 The traditional terminology of which sport, when translated into French, includes 'le guardien de guichet' and the abbreviation 'j.d.g.' representing 'jambe devant guichet'?

Three bonus questions on angles

a. What name is given to the steepest angle of descent, or the dip of a slope relative to the horizontal plane, at which material on the slope face is on the verge of sliding?

b. In geometric optics, what term is used for the angle that a ray or beam of radiation makes with a line perpendicular to the surface at the point of arrival?

c. Named after a Dutch physicist, which law states that the ratio of the sine of the angle of incidence to the sine of the angle of refraction is constant when a light ray passes from one medium to another?

6 A river, Christmas, a moon and a pair of shoes all share what colour, according to Elvis Presley?

Three bonus questions on a country

a. Mario Vargas Llosa, the winner of the 2010 Nobel Prize for Literature, stood for the presidency of which country, his birthplace, in 1990?

b. Jorge Chavez Airport in Lima is named after the pilot who, in 1910, flew from Brig to Domodossola over the Simplon Pass, making the first air crossing of which mountains?

c. Although known by an English name following his arrival in London, which figure in children's fiction was known as Pastuso in his native Peru?

7 First performed in 1958, which play by Shelagh Delaney concerns a working-class girl from Salford who becomes pregnant after a one-night stand?

Three bonus questions on tributaries of the River Thames. In each case, give the tributary whose name corresponds to the following.

a. A river whose name rhymes with the surname of the heroine of *Pride and Prejudice*?

b. A town in East Lancashire, part of the borough of Pendle along with Nelson and Barnoldswick?

c. A timid, home-loving animal, the first character to be introduced in a novel of 1908?

8 Published by HM Stationery Office and appearing in print daily, weekly, and online, the official reports of the proceedings of the Westminster Parliament are known by what name?

Three bonus questions on Parliament

a. Usually a Member of Parliament, the holder of which office is the government's principal legal adviser, the role involving civil law functions and final responsibility for criminal law?

b. Dating to 1415, which officer ensures the order and security of the House of Commons, and is the only person allowed to carry a sword there?

c. The holder of which office acts as custodian of the Great Seal of the Realm, and is the Secretary of State for Justice?

9 The engineers Sir James Martin and Valentine Baker made significant contributions to the design and development of which emergency device, their company having supplied the invention to over ninety air forces since the 1940s?

Three bonus questions on a name

a. What name, used in Germany as a title of nobility, is the title of a 1964 novel by Saul Bellow consisting partly of letters written by the central character?

b. The Franco-German author Emile Herzog is better known by what pen name, under which he wrote the 1923 book *Ariel* about the poet Shelley?

c. Which 1979 film by the director Werner Herzog starred Bruno Ganz and Klaus Kinski, and was an homage to a 1922 classic of German cinema directed by F.W. Murnau?

10 The six-letter name of which African country is an anagram of a word describing a clock that shows the time by means of a pointer or dial?

Three bonus questions on women in the ancient world, in the words of the author Charlotte Higgins. In each case, identify the mythological figure from her description.

a. '[In] Sophocles's play ... she gives her brother, who died a traitor, his proper funeral rites ... a standard-bearer for courage in the face of brutish male authority.'

b. 'When [her husband] leaves her for a younger model, she delivers a ... speech on the lot of married women, culminating in the ... line: "I'd rather stand in the battle line three times than give birth once."'

c. 'In the *Odyssey*, [she] turned visiting men into pigs. What more can I say?'

11 Ignoring accents, the names of two of the first eight months of the year may be transformed into their French equivalents by the substitution of a single letter. For ten points, name both.

Three bonus questions on Italian composers

a. Orfeo is among the compositions of which key figure in the early development of opera? He was Maestro di Capella at St Mark's Basilica in Venice from 1613 to 1643.

b. Born in 1602 in the Republic of Venice, which composer was an assistant organist under Monteverdi and wrote a number of operas including *Didone*, *Erismena* and *Calisto*?

c. Which Venetian composer made his first known public appearance as a violinist at St Mark's Basilica in 1696? He is best known for his concertos, of which around 500 survive.

12 Nantwich Town, Truro City and Whitley Bay are among recent winners of which football competition? It replaced the FA Amateur Cup in 1974.

Three bonus questions on mountains

a. Mount Logan, which rises to almost 6,000 metres in the St Elias Mountains, is the highest mountain in which country?

b. Mount Robson and Mount Columbia are peaks in which Canadian mountain range, an extension of a range that stretches along the border between Alberta and British Columbia?

c. Which formation within the Canadian Rockies, close to the town of Field in the Yoho National Park, is one of the world's most significant fossil fields?

13 'The liberties of England and the Protestant religion I will maintain.' Which royal figure made this claim when he landed at Brixham in Devon in 1688?

Three bonus questions on parts of the human body

a. Where on the body does a thin fold known as the eponychium extend over a crescent-shaped area called the lunula?

b. Also called the 'infra-nasal depression', what name is given to the vertical groove on the surface of the upper lip, below the septum of the nose?

c. A literal translation from the Latin, 'nares' is an alternative name for what part of the body?

14 '[It] consists in doing and saying things that cause shame to the victim, simply for the pleasure of it.' These words form part of Aristotle's definition of what six-letter term? In modern usage, it describes an excess of pride or ambition that ultimately causes the ruin of the perpetrator.

Three bonus questions on taxonomy

a. In 1990, which US microbiologist proposed a system of biological classification based on genetic relationships that divided all organisms into three domains?

b. Its name reflecting their ancient lineage, which domain contains methanogens, extremophiles and other microorganisms with distinctive membrane and cell wall structures?

c. Containing plants and animals, which domain is characterised by organisms whose cells contain structures enclosed within membranes?

15 Believing that knowledge evolves from experience of the mind, which Austrian-born philosopher formulated the principle of 'falsifiability' and published his first major work, *The Logic of Scientific Discovery*, in 1934?

Three bonus questions on environmental bodies

a. Established in 1988 by the United Nations Environment Programme and the World Meteorological Organization, what is the full name of the body usually known by the initials IPCC?

b. The European Environment Agency operational since 1994 has its headquarters in which European capital, the site of the 2009 United Nations Climate Change Conference?

c. In 2005, which non-governmental organisation launched a campaign called the Big Ask, calling for a new climate-change law in the UK?

16 Which national newspaper established itself in the market in the 1850s by undercutting other dailies in price and becoming London's first penny daily newspaper? Its political views were originally radical, and only later did it come to be regarded as embodying the outlook of conservative 'middle England'.

Three bonus questions on people whose names begin with the name of a Greek letter; for example, 'Rhodes' begins with 'Rho'. In each case, simply give the Greek letter.

a. The authors of *The Tale of Genji*, *An Unofficial Rose* and *Para Handy and Other Tales*

b. The three artists who painted *The Baptism of Christ*, *The Boulevard Montmartre by Night* and *Child with a Dove*?

    c. The wife of King Edward the Third and the husband of Queen Mary the First?

17 In the nineteenth century, which pair of writers wrote both the German dictionary *Deutsches Wörterbuch* and a series of stories published in the collection *Household Tales*, the first of which is usually known as 'The Frog King'?

> **Three bonus questions on medicine. In each case, give the common name for the diseases caused by the following microorganisms.**
>
> **a.** The two-word common name of *Bordetella pertussis*?
>
> **b.** *Treponema pallidum pallidum*?
>
> **c.** *Varicella-zoster* virus?

18 One of the Archimedean solids, a cuboctahedron has six equal square faces joined at the corners and connected by eight of which plane figure?

> **Three bonus questions on national parks**
>
> **a.** The first Scottish national park was established in 2002, covering Loch Lomond and which wooded glen near Loch Katrine?
>
> **b.** There are three national parks in Wales. The Brecon Beacons and Snowdonia are two; which is the third?
>
> **c.** Created in 1954, which national park lies primarily within Somerset and shares its name with a native pony characterised by a winter coat that is able to repel rain?

19 What five-letter word may indicate a number of different plants, including a lily regarded as sacred in ancient Egypt, an aquatic perennial with edible rhizomes used in Asian cuisine, and a legendary fruit that induced a state of dreamy forgetfulness, for example, in Homer's *Odyssey*?

Three bonus questions on a banking scandal

a. In 1838, John Sadleir founded a bank bearing the name of which large Irish county? He became an MP, embezzled more than £200,000 and, in 1856, was found dead on Hampstead Heath, alongside a vial of prussic acid.

b. Mr Merdle, a politician allegedly based on Sadleir, takes his life after the crash 'of a certain bank' in which novel by Charles Dickens?

c. Also thought to be based on Sadleir, the financier and MP Augustus Melmotte kills himself with prussic acid in the 1875 novel *The Way We Live Now*. Who was the author?

20 How many electrons does an atom of a halogen element have in its outer 'p' subshell?

Three bonus questions on botanical terms

a. Originally meaning a shoot or a twig, especially one cut to form a graft, what word also means an heir or a descendant, particularly of a noble house?

b. Used in electronics for a point in a circuit where several conductors meet, what word is also used in botany for the point on a stem from which a leaf or branch grows?

c. Used for the result of oxidation on iron, what term is also applied to a fungal infection causing reddish-brown spots on the leaves or stems of plants?

21 Given two points in the plane, with coordinates one comma ten and two comma nine, what is the length of the shortest path between them?

Three bonus questions on scientific terminology

a. 'I have taken your advice, and the names used are "anode", "cathode", "anions", "cations" and "ions".' These are the words of which English chemist and physicist, writing in 1834 to acknowledge terms suggested by the philosopher William Whewell?

b. In 1832, Whewell coined the terms 'uniformitarians' and 'catastrophists' for those with contending viewpoints in which science?

c. Also in 1834, Whewell wrote of 'the want of any name by which we can designate the students of the knowledge of the material world collectively'. What term, now in universal use, did he coin to address this lack?

22 Ten of Canada's thirteen provinces and territories are larger than the UK; for ten points, name two of the three that are smaller.

Three bonus questions on artists

a. The Ghent altarpiece has been attributed to two Flemish siblings, Hubert and Jan, who share what surname? The latter's works also include *Portrait of a Man in a Turban*, now in the National Gallery.

b. What was the surname of the eighteenth-century Venetian artist who was the brother-in-law of Francesco and Gian-Antonio Guardi and the father of two brothers, Gian-Domenico and Lorenzo, all of whom were painters?

c. A 'brother' in the religious sense, the Dominican Fra Giovanni da Fiesole, whose works include the frescoes in the Friary of San Marco in Florence, is usually known by what name or epithet?

'If you are lucky enough to have lived in Paris as a young man, then wherever you go for the rest of your life, it stays with you, for Paris is a moveable feast.' These are the words of which US novelist, who died in 1961?

Three bonus questions on the Indian Ocean

a. Which sea of the Indian Ocean is bounded to the north by the Irrawaddy Delta and takes its name from the islands that form part of the archipelago separating the sea from the Bay of Bengal?

b. Rising in Zambia, which is the largest African river to empty into the Indian Ocean, which it does in Mozambique?

c. The Mozambique Channel is an arm of the Indian Ocean that separates which large island from the eastern coast of mainland Africa?

 October 2011 saw the announcement of the winner of a competition organised by the Royal Institute of British Architects, the National Grid and the Department of Energy and Climate Change to find a new design for what ubiquitous structures?

Three bonus questions on Hamburgers

a. Forty operas and oratorios and the overture known as the *Water Music* are among the works of which composer? An influence on Handel, he was the music director of Hamburg's five main churches from 1721 until his death in 1767.

b. Born in Hamburg in 1809, which composer's work includes the *Reformation* and *Scottish* symphonies?

c. The *Academic Festival Overture* and the *German Requiem*, first performed in 1869, are among the works of which Hamburg-born composer?

25 In physics, the hyperfine coupling constant, magnetic vector potential, unit cell length, mass number and a factor of 10 to the minus 18 can all be indicated by what letter of the alphabet?

Three bonus questions on deaths with a shared location

a. What popular four-word name was given to the case of the bigamist George Joseph Smith who, in 1915, was convicted of murdering his three wives? They were found dead in different parts of the country, but in the same part of each house.

b. Charlotte Corday, who killed the French revolutionary leader Jean Paul Marat in his bath in 1793, was a member of which republican party, named after a region of France?

c. The son of Marcus Aurelius, which Roman emperor was reputedly strangled in his bath by his wrestling partner Narcissus, after his mistress's attempt to poison him failed?

26 Which vole-like arctic rodents are noted for their mass migrations in search of food during population explosions, giving rise to the much-repeated idea that they flock to the sea to drown themselves?

Three bonus questions on China

a. More than 4,500 kilometres in length, China's longest land frontier is with which country?

b. China's shortest land frontier, around 76 kilometres in length, is with which Central Asian country?

c. China shares borders of around 1,700 kilometres in total with which two landlocked Himalayan countries?

27 Warden Gad Hassan in *The Mummy*, a slave trader in *Gladiator*, Mr Safir in *Sex and the City 2* and the title role of Mahmud Nasir in *The Infidel* are among the film roles of which British-Iranian stand-up comedian?

Three bonus questions on genetic engineering

a. What name was given to the first mammal to be cloned from adult somatic cells, in 1996?

b. Dolly was produced by somatic cell nuclear transfer. In this technique, the nucleus from a somatic cell is transferred to what type of recipient cell?

c. What tissue was the source of the nucleus transferred to an embryonic cell to produce Dolly?

28 Meanings of what four-letter word include 'coarse file with separate teeth' and 'hoarse, grating sound'? Etymologically unrelated, the same four-letter word also begins the common name of the fruit of the bramble *Rubus idaeus*.

Three bonus questions on a European city

a. The Red Cross was founded in the 1860s in which European city, which later became the headquarters of the League of Nations?

b. Which philosopher and political theorist was born in Geneva in 1712 and wrote several of his major works there, including *Discourses on the Origin of Inequality* in 1755?

c. Based near Geneva, the Organisation Européene pour la Recherche Nucléaire is commonly known by what acronym, formed from its earlier full name?

29 Collagen is the constituent protein of which strong flexible connective tissue that joins bone to bone at moveable joints?

Three bonus questions on literary figures born in 1911. In each case, identify the author of the works listed

a. *The Spire, Pincher Martin* and *Rites of Passage*?

b. *Titus Groan, Gormenghast* and *Titus Alone*?

c. *The Night of the Iguana, The Rose Tattoo* and *Cat on a Hot Tin Roof*?

30 Which environmental activist died in Nairobi in September 2011? The founder of the Green Belt movement, in 2004 she became the first African woman to win the Nobel Prize for Peace.

Three bonus questions on US presidential running mates

a. Whom did Ronald Reagan choose as his running mate in 1980? He had formerly been a Texas congressman, an ambassador to the United Nations and a director of the CIA.

b. In 1988, George Bush Senior picked as his running mate which gaffe-prone senator? Noted for misspelling the word 'potato', he was upbraided in a vice-presidential debate when he compared himself to 'Jack' Kennedy.

c. In 1992, Bill Clinton chose which future Nobel Prize winner to be his running mate?

The Answers

1 Earnshaw's Theorem (Samuel Earnshaw, 1805–1888)
   a.   Globe (accept map of Eurasia and Africa)
   b.   Austria
   c.   Aeroflot

2 Ten (this is the binomial coefficient 5c3)
   a.   *Hamlet* (Claudius in IV.5)
   b.   *Richard the Second* (King in III.2)
   c.   *Romeo and Juliet* (Juliet in II.2)

3 Horsetail / mare's tail (also known as snake grass, puzzle grass)
   a.   Master of the King's Musick
   b.   (Sir) Peter Maxwell Davies
   c.   Prince Harry / Henry (of Wales)

4 Natterjack (toad)
   a.   150 million (so accept 140–160 million; more precisely 149.6 million)
   b.   30 (30.06 mean distance)
   c.   Voyager (or Voyager One / Voyager space probe)

5 Cricket ('wicket keeper' and 'leg before wicket')
   a.   (Critical) Angle of repose
   b.   Angle of incidence ('angle of attack' is somewhat different, and is used in aeronautics)
   c.   Snell's Law (Willebrord Snellius, 1580–1626; also called Descartes' Law, or Law of Refraction, but these do not answer the question)

6 Blue (as in suede shoes, of course)
- **a.** Peru
- **b.** The Alps (his plane crashed at the end and he died four days later)
- **c.** Paddington (Bear)

7 *A Taste of Honey*
- **a.** Kennet (Elizabeth Bennet)
- **b.** Colne (joins the Thames near Staines)
- **c.** Mole (*The Wind in the Willows*)

8 Hansard
- **a.** Attorney General
- **b.** Serjeant at Arms
- **c.** Lord Chancellor

9 Ejection seat
- **a.** Herzog
- **b.** André Maurois
- **c.** *Nosferatu* (*the Vampyre* ; the original German title of Herzog's film was *Nosferatu: Phantom der Nacht*; Murnau's was *Nosferatu, Eine Symphonie des Grauens*)

10 Angola (an anagram of 'analog', of course; this spelling is not restricted to US English)
- **a.** Antigone
- **b.** Medea
- **c.** Circe

11 April and May (Avril and Mai)
- **a.** (Claudio) Monteverdi
- **b.** (Francesco) Cavalli
- **c.** (Antonio) Vivaldi

12 The FA Vase / the Football Association Challenge Vase (not FA Trophy)

a. Canada
b. (Canadian) Rockies
c. Burgess shale (formation)

13 William of Orange / William the Third
a. On a fingernail
b. Philtrum
c. Nostrils / nasal passages (singular: naris, 'a nostril')

14 Hubris
a. (Carl Richard) Woese
b. Archaea / Archae(o)bacteria
c. Eucarya / Eukaryota / Eukaryotes

15 (Sir Karl) Popper (NB 1934 is the date of the original German publication not the English translation – with the English title – which came out in 1959)
a. Intergovernmental Panel on Climate Change
b. Copenhagen
c. Friends of the Earth

16 (*Daily*) *Telegraph* (NB the *Daily Mail* was founded later, in 1896)
a. Mu (Murasaki, Murdoch, Munro)
b. Pi (Piero della Francesca, Pissarro and Picasso)
c. Phi (Philippa of Hainault, Philip II)

17 The Brothers Grimm (Jacob, 1785–1863; Wilhelm, 1786–1859)
a. Whooping cough
b. Syphilis
c. Chickenpox (accept shingles)

18 (Equilateral) Triangle
a. The Trossachs (Loch Lomond and the Trossachs National Park)
b. Pembrokeshire Coast (National Park)
c. Exmoor (not Dartmoor, which is entirely in Devon)

19 Lotus
   a. Tipperary (Joint Stock Bank)
   b. *Little Dorrit*
   c. (Anthony) Trollope

20 Five
   a. Scion
   b. Node
   c. Rust

21 Square root of 2 (accept 1.414 or root 2; the shortest path is the straight line between these two points. According to Pythagoras' theorem, the square of the length of this line equals (1 - 2)2 + (10 - 9) 2 = 1 + 1 = 2; (1, 10), (2, 9))
   a. (Michael) Faraday
   b. Geology
   c. Scientist

22 Nova Scotia, New Brunswick, Prince Edward
   a. Van Eyck (There is some doubt whether Hubert actually existed)
   b. Tiepolo (Giovanni Battista [Giambattista] Tiepolo)
   c. Fra Angelico

23 (Ernest) Hemingway
   a. Andaman Sea
   b. Zambezi
   c. Madagascar

24 (Electricity) Pylons (won by Danish engineering firm Bystrup for their design for the 'T-Pylon')
   a. (Georg Philipp) Telemann
   b. (Felix) Mendelssohn
   c. (Johannes) Brahms

25 A (for Alpha)
   a. 'Brides in the Bath'

   b.   Girondins or Girondist

   c.   Commodus (Lucius Aurelius Commodus Antoninus,
            AD 161–192)

26 Lemmings (*Lemmus lemmus*)
   a.   Mongolia
   b.   Afghanistan
   c.   Nepal and Bhutan

27 Omid Djalili
   a.   Dolly (the sheep)
   b.   (Denucleated) Embryonic cell
   c.   Mammary gland (she was named after Dolly Parton)

28 Rasp (raspberry)
   a.   Geneva
   b.   (Jean-Jacques) Rousseau
   c.   Cern (formerly Conseil Européen pour la Recherche
            Nucléaire')

29 Ligament
   a.   (William) Golding (1911–1993)
   b.   (Mervyn) Peake (1911–1968)
   c.   Tennessee Williams (1911–1983)

30 Wangari Maathai
   a.   George H.W. Bush (George Bush Senior)
   b.   Dan Quayle (James Danforth Quayle)
   c.   Al Gore (Albert Arnold Gore, Jr.)

Match Three

1 Which Italian city links: a school of painting whose members included the Caracci family; a large sausage made of mixed meat, and a meat-based pasta sauce usually known in Italian as 'ragu'?

Three bonus questions on Scottish literature

a. Subtitled *A Life in Four Books* and including his own illustrations, *Lanark* is a work of 1981 by which author?

b. Which Scottish writer and comedian won the 2007 Costa prize for the novel *Day*? Her other works include *On Bullfighting* and *Paradise*.

c. Making her debut in 1997 with *Like*, which Scottish writer's novel *The Accidental* was short-listed for the Booker Prize in 2005?

2 Born in 1870, which Swedish mathematician gives his name to the 'star', 'snowflake' or 'island' that is one of the earliest described types of fractal curve?

Three bonus questions on religious agreements

a. What word is used in English bibles for a contract with God such as that made at Mount Sinai, when Israel agreed to obey God's laws after he freed them from slavery?

b. In 1638, members of which Protestant Scottish church, named after their council of elders, signed a 'National Covenant' to protect their form of worship?

c. What four-word name was given to the agreement between the English Parliament and the Scots in 1643 to strengthen their position against Charles the First?

3 Quote: 'All national institutions of churches ... appear to me no other than human inventions, set up to terrify and enslave mankind, and monopolise power and profit.' These are the words of which radical author, in the 1794 work *The Rights of Man*?

Three bonus questions on political entities whose names begin with the word 'Northern'. In each case, give the two-word name from the description.

a. A self-governing territory of the USA in the Western Pacific; its largest island is Saipan.

b. The name by which Zambia was known before independence in 1964?

c. A de facto state established in 1974 following intervention by the Turkish army?

4 The orbit of which planet of the Solar System has the least pronounced eccentricity, that is, its orbit is most nearly a true circle?

Three bonus questions on the French revolutionary calendar

a. Bastille Day fell in the month named Messidor, which has what meaning in English?

b. Instead of weeks, every month was organised into three groups of ten days known as what?

c. The month running from the middle of March to the middle of April gave its name to a novel of 1885 by which writer?

(5) The kitemark, familiar as a UK-registered certification symbol of quality and safety, is enclosed at its base by two lines in the shape of a letter 'V'. Which two letters appear at the top?

Three bonus questions on Australian marsupials

a. Inhabiting the coastal scrub of both Australia and New Guinea, a pademelon is a small species of which marsupial?

b. Which large, nocturnal, burrowing marsupial has three species: the common, the southern hairy-nosed, and the northern hairy-nosed?

c. In 2010, Australian scientists announced that they had taught the quoll, an endangered cat-sized marsupial, to suppress its instinct to eat which invasive, toxic amphibians?

(6) Answer promptly if you buzz for this. Give all five of the three-letter words which differ only in their middle letters and mean, in reverse alphabetical order, greyish-brown, a Spanish nobleman, a loud noise, an animal's lair, and a level of proficiency in karate?

Three bonus questions on a shape

a. In Cartesian coordinates, what shape is the solution to the equation $1 - x2 - y2 - z2 = 0$?

b. Which British-born US physicist gives his name to a 'sphere' that is a vast arrangement of artificial habitats orbiting a star, which he proposed as an observable signature of extraterrestrial civilisations?

c. Being a planet's gravitational region of influence, what 'sphere' is named after a US astronomer born in 1838?

7 What number results if you add together: the traditional number of Garibaldi's volunteers in 1860; the Light Brigade according to Tennyson; the 'Blows' in the title of Truffaut's film; Aeschylus's champions against Thebes; and the number of platonic solids?

Three bonus questions on sport

a. What is the nationality of the tennis player Novak Djokovic? He was the first player from his country to win a Grand Slam when he won the Australian Open in 2008.

b. Which Serbian football club is the only one from that country to have won a UEFA competition?

c. Serbia won the 2009 World Championship in which aquatic team sport, admitted to the Olympics at the 1900 games?

8 In finance, what Italian-derived term refers to unsecured, higher-yielding loans that are often used to fund takeovers? In more general usage, it denotes a low storey between two others in a building, typically between the ground and first floors.

Three bonus questions on entries from the Wikipedia page 'Lamest edit wars', a list of topics that have provoked needless controversy. Name the person whose 'edit war' may be summarised as follows. In each case, the answer is a single surname.

a. 'Should this surname redirect to the page of a US politician or to that of a member of the Monty Python team?'

b. 'What demonym describes this scientist? Born of Serbian parents in a part of the Austrian empire, which a short time later became a part of the Hungarian half of Austria-Hungary and is now in Croatia. He later became a US citizen.'

c. 'How is the surname pronounced? Does it rhyme with "foaling", or does it rhyme with "howling"?'

9 Roquet, peel and cannon are strokes, and a bisque is a free turn, in which game that featured in the 1900 Olympics and has a world series for the MacRobertson Shield?

Three bonus questions on scientific terms, specifically, those that can be made from the seven letters of the word 'gondola'. In each case, give the word from the description.

a. An animal organ that secretes substances for use in the body, for example, the thyroid?

b. Pertaining to the joint of a stem, or the part where a leaf or several leaves are inserted, or to a point of intersection in general?

c. The three-letter short form of a term meaning 'power to which a fixed number of base must be raised to produce a given number'?

10 Of the landlocked countries of Europe, which is the largest, being around four-fifths the size of the UK?

Three bonus questions on signal processing

a. What term can mean both varying an electromagnetic wave in order to impress a signal on it, and a change of key in a piece of music?

b. From the Greek for 'different power', what term refers to the generation of beat frequencies by the combination of two waveforms?

c. Including Hannibal Lecter among its devotees and notably used in the theme music for *Midsomer Murders*, what musical instrument, named after its Russian inventor, uses the heterodyne principle to generate tones based on the movement of the musician's hands near two antennas?

11 What everyday word can precede 'law', 'sense' and 'market', the latter expression indicating the international institution that the UK joined in 1973?

Three bonus questions on invertebrates

a. What common name is given to the many thousands of species of invertebrates whose scientific name, *Annelida*, comes from the Latin for 'little ring'?

b. Also known as roundworms, which unsegmented worms are parasites of plants and animals and are added to soil by gardeners as an organic slug killer?

c. The parasitic *Hirudo medicinalis* is a species of which annelids? They secrete the anti-clotting enzyme hirudin into their host's blood stream.

12 Listen carefully. When read aloud, the three words meaning 'island whose capital is Douglas', 'units of digital information' and 'common name of *Canis lupus familiaris*' form what improbable three-word headline, a well-known journalistic aphorism?

Three bonus questions on the works of Goethe. In each case, identify the title character of the work described.

a. An epistolary novel of 1774, in which a sensitive artist is driven to destruction by his unrequited love for the young Charlotte?

b. An historical play about a Flemish nobleman beheaded in 1568 after defying the King of Spain; Beethoven later wrote an overture and incidental music for it?

c. A poetic drama in two parts that begins with Mephistopheles seeking permission in Heaven to attempt the ruin of the title character's soul?

13 The first British cyclist in 46 years to win the World Road Racing Championship, and the first ever to win the Tour de France Green Jersey for Top Sprinter, who was voted BBC Sports Personality of the Year in December 2011?

Three bonus questions on short stories

a. The 1999 collection *Close Range: Wyoming Stories*, which includes the story 'Brokeback Mountain', is by which US author?

b. 'The Sacrificial Egg' and 'Girls at War' are among the short stories of which Nigerian author, born in 1930?

c. Which author wrote *Notwithstanding*, a 2009 book of stories about a fictional English village? Settings of his novels include Latin America, Australia, Turkey and the island of Cephalonia.

14 Also called white mica, which pale, translucent, potassium-containing mineral of the mica group shares its name with a native or inhabitant of the capital of the Russian Federation?

Three bonus questions on archaeologists

a. Leonard Woolley directed the excavations at what site in Mesopotamia in the 1920s, his discoveries including the copper bull of the third millennium BC, now on display at the British Museum?

b. Having surveyed Stonehenge, which archaeologist turned to Egyptology from 1881? He began by surveying Giza and excavating the mounds of Tanis and Naucratis.

c. Arthur Evans excavated the Bronze Age city of Knossos and, in 1904, discovered the remains of the civilisation to which he gave what name?

15 In trigonometry, which function of an angle in a right-angled triangle can be found by dividing the length of the side adjacent to the angle by the length of the hypotenuse?

Three bonus questions on the sciences

a. Messier Object number one is a nebula in Taurus believed to be the remnant of a supernova observed in 1054 by Chinese and Arabian astronomers, and has what common name, referring to its shape?

b. The crab family *Ocypodidae* includes the ghost crabs and a genus given what common name, after the characteristic up-and-down motion of the small claw against the large claw when feeding?

c. George Crabbe, the English poet and naturalist, was the author in 1790 of an essay on the natural history of which region on the borders of Leicestershire, Nottinghamshire and Lincolnshire?

16 Sometimes called the pallium, the layer of epidermal tissue that encloses the body of a mollusc and secretes the shell is commonly known by what name, originally meaning a cloak? In geology, it denotes the Earth's interior between the crust and the core.

Three bonus questions on Greek nymphs

a. What collective name was given to the fifty daughters of the goddess Doris, derived from that of their father, who is sometimes referred to as 'the Old Man of the Sea'?

b. The nereid Amphitrite became the wife of which of the Greek gods, to whom she bore the son Triton?

c. The nereid Thetis married Peleus and became the mother of which Greek hero?

17 What letter precedes 'factor' in the name of a parameter that describes, in electronics, the ratio of the reactance of an inductor or capacitor to its series resistance and, more generally, the under-damping of an oscillatory system, expressing a relationship between stored energy and energy dissipation?

Three bonus questions on geography. In each case, name the island whose largest town or city is the following. The islands in question are among the world's ten largest.

a. Medan, with a population of around two million?

b. Iqaluit, with a population of around 6,000?

c. Antananarivo, with an estimated population of one million?

18 Used in acoustics and telecommunications to indicate the degree to which a sound or picture reproduced or transmitted by any device resembles the original, what word is used in a more general sense to mean faithfulness and loyalty?

Three bonus questions on inventions. In each case, give the decade of the twentieth century in which the following were invented.

a. Liposuction, the laser printer, 'post-it' notes and magnetic resonance imaging?

b. Astroturf, the hover mower, the cash dispenser and silicone breast implants?

c. The lie detector, the medical dressing 'Elastoplast', bubble gum, and the commercially manufactured car radio?

19 Which nineteenth-century poet wrote the following: 'The lark's on the wing; / The snail's on the thorn; / God's in His heaven — / All's right with the world!'?

Three bonus questions on an area of outstanding natural beauty

a. Designated an area of outstanding natural beauty in 1964, which moorland region of fells and valleys covers about 300 square miles, mainly in Lancashire?

b. Following his defeat at Hexham, which monarch was living in secret at Waddington Hall in the Forest of Bowland when he was betrayed and taken into custody?

c. Reaching over 1,800 feet above the eastern part of the Ribble Valley, which hill of Bowland lies detached from the Forest and was the home of around a dozen people tried in 1612 on charges of murder by witchcraft?

20 Originally the name of a political club founded in 1659 by James Harrington, what term for a list of names and duties is taken from the Latin for 'wheel'?

Three bonus questions on UN peacekeeping operations

a. The observer group UNOGIL was deployed in 1958 to which Eastern Mediterranean country? In 1978, the UN interim force UNIFIL was also deployed there.

b. UNIPOM was a UN observation mission established in which two Asian countries from 1965 to 1966, to supervise the ceasefire along their shared border?

c. The UN force called UNFICYP has operated on which Mediterranean island since 1964, to supervise ceasefire lines and maintain a buffer zone?

21 Although its origins can be traced to French doctors in the 1920s, what term has also been credited to the New York beauty salon owner Nicole Ronsard, who in 1973 wrote a book about diet-resistant fat deposits that give the skin a dimpled appearance?

Three bonus questions on a German chemist

a. A milestone in organic chemistry, in 1828 Friedrich Woehler synthesised what substance, hitherto considered a purely animal product? It has the molecular formula CH_4N_2O.

b. At around the same time, Woehler isolated two metallic elements, with the atomic numbers 4 and 13. For five points, name both.

c. In 1862, Woehler discovered the reaction of calcium carbide with water, producing which colourless hydrocarbon gas, formula C_2H_2?

22 In 1611, the Civic Guard of Antwerp commissioned which Flemish artist to create the 'Descent from the Cross' triptych for their altar in the city's cathedral?

Three bonus questions on major cities. In each case, name the city in which the following districts are located

a. Mayfair, Civic Betterment, Swampoodle, the Palisades and Foggy Bottom?

b. Santa Cruz, Cotton Green, Aarey Milk Colony, Seven Bungalows and Film City?

c. Booterstown, Leopardstown, Swords, the Liberties and Chapelizod?

23 Which three-letter Latin word can be concatenated with the letters r-k to give one of the smallest known physical objects, and with the letters s-a-r to give one of the largest known physical objects?

Three bonus questions on an English poet and dramatist

a. A reworking of Shakespeare's *Antony and Cleopatra, All for Love* is a work by which Restoration author?

b. Which poem of 1681 by Dryden adapts a story from the Old Testament to satirise the role of Lord Shaftesbury and the Duke of Monmouth in the Exclusion Crisis?

c. Set in Sicily, which comedy of 1673 by Dryden shares its title with a later series of six paintings by William Hogarth, now in the National Gallery?

24 In units of ideal gas constant r, what is the molar heat capacity of an ideal monatomic gas?

Three bonus questions on cities in Wales

a. Kingsley Amis's novel *The Old Devils* is usually thought to be set in which Welsh city, where the author was a lecturer during the 1950s?

b. In which Welsh city is John Frost Square, named after the leader of a Chartist 'uprising' of 1839 in which around twenty people were killed by armed soldiers?

c. In addition to Cardiff, Swansea and Newport, two other communities in Wales have city status. For five points, name either.

25 Excluding the sex chromosomes, how many matched pairs of chromosomes are there in a normal human somatic cell?

Three bonus questions on English words that derive from Arabic. In each case give the word from the definition.

a. From an Arabic word meaning 'reunion of broken parts', the branch of mathematics that deals with the study of the rules of operations and relations?

b. From the name of a ninth-century Persian mathematician, a set of steps or instructions designed to solve a problem?

c. From an Arabic term referring to powdered antimony used as eye make-up, a colourless, volatile liquid that may be used as an industrial solvent and as fuel?

26 In the measurement of geological time, what is the first subdivision of an aeon, consisting of periods of several hundred million years? An example would be the Cenozoic.

Three bonus questions on a river

a. In *The Waste Land*, which river does T.S. Eliot describe as 'sweet', urging it to 'run softly till I end my song, / ... run softly, for I speak not loud nor long'?

b. Which novel by Dickens, published from 1864 to 1865, opens with a scavenger and his daughter in a boat at night on the Thames?

c. A boat anchored in the Thames Estuary is the setting for Marlow's recollection of his experiences on the River Congo in which novella of 1902?

27 His seven 'opponents' having devoted much of their campaigns to praising his rule, President Berdymukhamedhov captured ninety-seven per cent of the vote in an election of February 2012 to win a new five-year term as ruler of which Central Asian state?

Three bonus questions on illustrators

a. From 1935 to 1965, Alfred Bestall wrote and illustrated eponymous stories of which children's character, who first appeared in the *Daily Express* in 1920?

b. Pauline Baynes illustrated the works of Tolkien and a *Dictionary of Chivalry*, for which she won the Kate Greenaway Medal, but is perhaps better known for her work on which series of novels published between 1950 and 1956?

c. Thomas Henry is noted for his illustrations, between 1921 and 1964, of works featuring which fictional schoolboy and his friends Ginger, Henry and Douglas?

28 In which country is Cape Piai the southernmost point of mainland Asia?

Three bonus questions on food safety and hygiene

a. The Codex Alimentarius Commission develops internationally recognised food safety standards and practices, and was established in 1963 by the World Health Organization and which agency of the United Nations?

b. A system of food safety management that identifies problems and preventative procedures, for what do the letters H.A.C.C.P. stand?

c. Belonging to the family *Caliciviridae*, which RNA virus causes the common gastroenteritis known as 'winter vomiting disease'?

29 Described as 'the hero among those third-rate men', which character in Thackeray's *Vanity Fair* dies at the Battle of Waterloo soon after marrying Amelia Sedley? He shares his name with a prominent member of the Cameron governments in the UK since 2010.

Three bonus questions on an element

a. Which element, obtained by electrolysis of its chloride from seawater, is used in alloys for its lightness, and in flashbulbs because of its exothermic reaction with oxygen?

b. Magnesium is always found combined in nature, mainly as a carbonate in magnesite and in which other mineral, sharing its name with a European mountain range?

c. Hydrated magnesium sulphate, which occurs as a mineral in a spring in Surrey, is commonly given what name when it is sold medicinally as a relaxant and a laxative?

30 Which twelfth-century Welsh chronicler and churchman was the author of *The History of the Kings of Britain*?

Three bonus questions on language and literature

a. 'The invention of languages is the foundation. The "stories" were made rather to provide a world for the languages than the reverse.' Referring to a major novel of 1954, which author said these words?

b. In an essay of 1955, Tolkien wrote that the English phrase 'cellar door' has great beauty, especially if dissociated from its sense, and that phrases of comparable beauty are 'extraordinarily frequent' in which Indo-European language?

c. 'It was like discovering a wine cellar filled with bottles of amazing wine of a kind and flavour never tasted before.' These words refer to Tolkien's discovery of which language, an official language of the EU since 1995?

The Answers

1 Bologna
- **a.** Alasdair Gray
- **b.** A.L. Kennedy (Alison Louise Kennedy)
- **c.** Ali Smith

2 (Helge von) Koch (1870–1924; *The Koch Snowflake*)
- **a.** Covenant
- **b.** Presbyterian
- **c.** Solemn League and Covenant

3 (Thomas) Paine
- **a.** Northern Marianas
- **b.** Northern Rhodesia
- **c.** Northern Cyprus

4 Venus (eccentricity of 0.0068)
- **a.** Harvest (Latin: *messis*, harvest)
- **b.** Décades (accept decades)
- **c.** Émile Zola (*Germinal*, of course)

5 B and S (for British Standards)
- **a.** Wallaby (scrub wallaby is the pademelon's alternative name)
- **b.** Wombat
- **c.** Cane toads

6 Dun, don, din, den, dan
- **a.** Sphere

b. Freeman Dyson (Dyson sphere)

c. Hill sphere (George William Hill; also known as the Roche sphere or lobe after Frenchman Edouard Roche)

7 2012 (Expedition of the Thousand, the six hundred, *Les Quatre Cent Coups*, *Seven Against Thebes*, five)

a. Serbian

b. Red Star Belgrade / F.K. Crvena Zvezda

c. Water polo

8 Mezzanine

a. Palin (i.e. should 'Palin' redirect to 'Sarah' or 'Michael'?)

b. (Nikola) Tesla

c. (J.K.) Rowling

9 Croquet

a. Gland

b. Nodal

c. Log

10 Belarus (Austria, Hungary, Czech Republic, Switzerland, etc. are all less than half the size of the UK)

a. Modulation

b. Heterodyning

c. Theremin (accept theremino-phone, theremin-vox; named after Professor Leon Theremin; also called the aetherphone but that doesn't answer the question)

11 Common

a. Earthworms (accept but qualify worms)

b. Nematodes

c. Leeches

12 Man Bites Dog ('man bytes dog')

a. (*The Sorrows of Young*) Werther

b. Egmont (Lamoral, Count of Egmont, 1522–1568)

c. Faust

13 Mark Cavendish
- **a.** (E.) Annie Proulx
- **b.** (Chinua) Achebe
- **c.** Louis de Bernières

14 Muscovite
- **a.** Ur
- **b.** (Sir William Matthew) Flinders Petrie
- **c.** Minoan

15 Cosine
- **a.** Crab (Nebula)
- **b.** Fiddler (crab)
- **c.** Vale of Belvoir

16 Mantle
- **a.** Nereids or nereides (from *nereus*)
- **b.** Poseidon
- **c.** Achilles

17 Q (for Quebec)
- **a.** Sumatra
- **b.** Baffin Island
- **c.** Madagascar

18 Fidelity
- **a.** 1970s
- **b.** 1960s
- **c.** 1920s

19 (Robert) Browning ('Pippa's Song')
- **a.** Forest of Bowland
- **b.** Henry the Sixth
- **c.** Pendle (Hill)

20 Rota

    a.   Lebanon
    b.   India and Pakistan
    c.   Cyprus

21 Cellulite
    a.   Urea (accept carbamide; not uric acid)
    b.   Beryllium and aluminium
    c.   Acetylene / ethyne

22 (Peter Paul) Rubens
    a.   Washington (DC)
    b.   Mumbai (accept Bombay)
    c.   Dublin

23 Qua (quark and quasar)
    a.   (John) Dryden
    b.   'Absalom and Achitophel' (from Samuel ii)
    c.   *Marriage à la Mode*

24 3 / 2 (r)
    a.   Swansea
    b.   Newport
    c.   St David's / Bangor

25 22
    a.   Algebra
    b.   Algorithm (Muhammad ibn Musa al Khwarizmi, c.780–850)
    c.   Alcohol

26 Era
    a.   River Thames
    b.   *Our Mutual Friend*
    c.   *Heart of Darkness* (by Joseph Conrad)

27 Turkmenistan

a. Rupert Bear
b. *The Chronicles of Narnia*
c. William (Brown, as in *Just William*, the first of the books)

28 Malaysia

a. Food and Agriculture Organisation / FAO
b. Hazard Analysis (and) Critical Control Points
c. Norovirus (accept Norwalk virus / Small Round Structured Viruses or S.R.S.V.)

29 George Osborne

a. Magnesium
b. Dolomite (both named after French geologist Déodat de Dolomieu. Also occurs in brucite and in others as a chloride or silicate)
c. Epsom salt(s) (not Andrews (liver) salts; not milk of magnesia, which is magnesium hydroxide)

30 Geoffrey of Monmouth

a. (J.R.R.) Tolkien
b. Welsh (in the essay 'English and Welsh', his valedictory address to Oxford University)
c. Finnish

Match Four

1. The early twentieth-century composers Tailleferre, Durey, Auric, Honegger, Poulenc and Milhaud are often referred to by what collective name, in French or in English?

   Three bonus questions on fictional books

   a.   Which animated television series has featured books entitled 'Great Machete Battles', 'Zapp Brannigan's Big Book of War' and 'Harry Potter and the Balance of Earth' by Al Gore?

   b.   'Ethel the Aardvark Goes Quantity-Surveying' and 'Thirty Days in the Samarkand Desert with the Duchess of Kent' are fictional titles in variations of a sketch devised by which BBC comedy team?

   c.   'Stu the Cockatoo Is New at the Zoo' by Sarah Carpenter is used by Sheldon Cooper as a guide to creating a flowchart in which US sitcom?

2. The pronuba moth is the sole pollinator of many species of which genus of perennial plants and trees native to arid parts of the Americas and distinguished by their sharp, sword-like leaves?

   Three bonus questions on the Seven Deadly Sins

   a.   In 'Purgatory', the second book of Dante's *Divine Comedy*, those guilty of which of the Seven Sins have had their eyes stitched and sealed with iron wire?

b. In the *Divine Comedy*, the penance for those guilty of which Sin is to run endlessly around the ledge of the Mountain of Purgatory to which they are confined?

c. Dante writes that those guilty of which Sin must pass through an immense wall of flame in the seventh and final terrace of the mountain?

3 'A thing of beauty is a joy for ever'; which Romantic poet wrote these words?

Three bonus questions on gases

a. In 1996, the Lawrence Livermore National Laboratory in California created the metallic form of which gas, originally discovered in 1766 by Henry Cavendish?

b. Which gas was discovered in 1898 by Sir William Ramsay and M.W. Travers in the residue of distilled liquid air? It is used in lightbulbs, lasers, and in arc lamps for cinema projection.

c. Pierre Janssen and Norman Lockyer are jointly credited with the detection in 1868 of which gas as an unexpected line in the Sun's spectrum? It was discovered on Earth in 1895 in the uranium mineral clevite.

4 An unusual combination in English, what two letters, both vowels, begin words meaning the principal and Turkic people of Western China, an Afrikaans word for a foreigner, and two islands of the western isles, separated from one another by Benbecula?

Three bonus questions on language

a. For which novel, written in Paris over a period of seventeen years and published as a whole in 1939, did its author invent an idioglossia, drawing on around forty different languages?

b. The US physicist Murray Gellman took the spelling of the elementary particle he called the quark from the line in *Finnegans Wake*: 'three quarks for muster mark'. What, in the context of the novel, is the immediate meaning of 'quark'?

c. Which term did the US anthropologist Joseph Campbell borrow from *Finnegans Wake* to denote the concept of the hero's journey, which is common to the epic works and folk tales of many cultures?

5 Sometimes confused with an expression of surprise or horror, for example on finding a cockroach in a bag of crisps, which three-letter palindrome means 'to make something last longer by supplementing it' or 'to make a living with difficulty'?

Three bonus questions on astronomy

a. 12.566 of what unit is equal to the entire celestial sphere?

b. Rounded to the nearest thousand, what is the total area of the sphere in square degrees?

c. As viewed from Earth, it would take 200,000 suns to cover the whole celestial sphere. What is the angular diameter of the Sun, to the nearest half a degree?

6 Signed on 25 March 1957, which treaty was the first and founding act of the European Economic Community?

Three bonus questions on damaged reputations

a. In which comedy by Sheridan do Lady Sneerwell, Mrs Candour and Sir Benjamin Backbite do their worst to damage as many reputations as possible?

b. Shortlisted for the 2003 Booker Prize, *Notes on a Scandal*, concerning a teacher's observations of her colleague's illicit affair, is by which British writer?

c. The 1989 film *Scandal* is based on the events surrounding the revelation in 1963 that which politician had had an affair with the model Christine Keeler?

7 Named after the French biologist who published it in the early 1800s, which now-discredited theory of biological evolution held that acquired characteristics resulting from an organism's response to environmental pressures can be inherited?

Three bonus questions on men born in the year 1829. In each case, identify the person from the description.

a. A founder of the Pre-Raphaelite brotherhood, whose works include *Christ in the House of his Parents* and *Bubbles*?

b. The father of the author of the *Mapp and Lucia* novels, who became Archbishop of Canterbury in 1882?

c. A religious leader who, in 1865, established a mission in the East End that later became the Salvation Army?

8 Particularly associated with continental Europe during the first half of the eighteenth century, which artistic style is thought to derive its name from either a French word for 'shellwork' or the Italian word for the earlier baroque period?

Three bonus questions on geophysics

a. What term describes the crust and brittle part of the upper mantle of a rocky planet when considered together?

b. What name is given to the region of the mantle directly beneath the lithosphere?

c. What theory, developed by Wegener, describes the dynamics of the lithosphere?

9 Listen carefully and answer as soon as your name is called. If the integers from one to one hundred are written in Roman numerals and then placed in alphabetical order, which comes last?

Three bonus questions on a prominent family

a. *The Last Empress* by Hannah Pakula is a biography of Soong May-Ling, who, in 1943, became only the second woman to address a joint session of the US Congress. To which political and military leader was she married?

b. Later a high-ranking figure in Communist China, May-Ling's older sister, Ch'ing-Ling, was the wife of which Chinese revolutionary, who died in 1925?

c. Ai-Ling, the oldest of the three sisters, was married to H.H. Kung. Said to have been the richest man in China, he held what office from 1933 to 1944?

10 'Population, when unchecked, increases in a geometrical ratio. Subsistence only increases in an arithmetical ratio.' Who wrote these words in his 'Essay on Population', published in 1798?

Three bonus questions on historic trials

a. Sometimes called the 'Monkey Trial', the historic case tried in Tennessee in 1925 is usually named after which high school teacher charged with teaching the theory of evolution?

b. The identity of which French peasant was the central issue of a trial held in 1560 in the town of Rieux in the South of France?

c.   Which locomotive won the Rainhill Trials during the
development of the Liverpool and Manchester Railway
in 1829?

11 What five-letter adjective is found in all the following:
the popular name for Charles the First's Parliament of
1640; another term for stenography; and an electrical
circuit that acts as a shunt to a circuit of comparatively
large resistance?

Three bonus questions on words indicating great size

a.   Which common adjective, now implying great size,
originally had the meaning of 'deviating from the
ordinary type'?

b.   Which synonym for 'colossal' comes from the Latin
word for 'unmeasurable'?

c.   Which word meaning 'very big' is derived from the
name of one of the title characters of a book published
in France in 1535?

12 Referring to a precise number of legs, which order
of crustacea includes shrimps, prawns, crabs and
lobsters?

Three bonus questions on foreign policy 'doctrines'

a.   Which Soviet leader gave his name to a foreign policy
'doctrine' by which the USSR reserved the right to use
military force to prevent its satellites from courses that
'damaged socialism'?

b.   After a popular US performer, what name did a Soviet
foreign ministry spokesman give to the USSR's policy
towards the 1989 revolutions in Eastern Europe?

c. Which US president's 'doctrine' was first announced with a speech to a joint session of Congress requesting $400 million in aid for Greece and Turkey, and a pledge 'to support free peoples'?

13 Tetracyclines and quinolones are classes of what general type of drug, originally derived from cultures of living organisms such as fungi?

Three bonus questions on plant cytology

a. What specific term denotes the soft-walled, undifferentiated cells that form the basic ground tissue of plants? They make up the bulk of non-woody structures such as pith and mesophyll.

b. From the Greek for 'divided', what term indicates plant tissue capable of undergoing mitosis, thus giving rise to new cells at the growing tips?

c. What term denotes the lateral meristems from which secondary growth arises, forming cork and vascular bundles?

14 Listen carefully. For which positive integers n does a real polynomial of degree n necessarily have a real root?

Three bonus questions on Young British Artists. In each case, name the artist from her works.

a. The monumental paintings *Plan* and *Torso Two*, and the triptych entitled *Strategy: South Face, Front Face, North Face*, which appeared on the cover of the Manic Street Preachers' album *The Holy Bible*?

b. The photographic series of 1992–1993 entitled *Signs that say what you want them to say and not signs that say what someone else wants you to say*?

c. The photographic series entitled *Naked Flame* and *Crying Men*, and the 2009 feature film *Nowhere Boy*?

15 Answer as soon as you buzz, and you can have two per cent either way. The University Boat Race course of 4 miles 374 yards represents what percentage of a standard marathon race?

> **Three bonus questions on figure skating. In each case, name the jump from the description.**
>
> **a.** The only jump that begins with the skater facing forward, it is launched on the forward outside edge of the skate and landed on the back outside edge of the opposite foot. A single variation involves the skater making one and a half revolutions in the air.
>
> **b.** Considered one of the easiest jumps, a single variation of this move involves the skater launching from the rear inside edge of one skate, making one full turn in the air, and landing on the rear outside edge of the opposite skate.
>
> **c.** A counter-rotated toe jump from the rear outside edge to the opposite rear outside edge, often preceded by a long backward diagonal glide.

16 According to Mercutio in Shakespeare's *Romeo and Juliet*, what is the name of the fairies' midwife, who 'comes in shape no bigger than an agate stone / On the fore-finger of an alderman', and who helps sleepers give birth to their dreams?

> **Three bonus questions on anachronisms in Shakespeare**
>
> **a.** In which of Shakespeare's plays does a clock strike and a character comment 'The clock has stricken three', although striking clocks were a later invention?

    b.   In which of the History Plays does the Duke of Gloucester boast that he could 'set the murderous Machiavel to school', despite Machiavelli not being born until several years later?

    c.   *Troilus and Cressida* is set during the Trojan War, so supposedly during the twelfth century BC, although Hector quotes which Greek philosopher of the fourth century BC, recounting his opinion that young men are 'unfit to hear moral philosophy'?

17 Quote: 'There exists a great background, vital and vivid, which matters more than the people who move upon it.' These words of D.H. Lawrence refer to the works of which novelist and poet, who died in 1928?

Three bonus questions on mottos

    a.   'Multum in parvo', meaning 'much in little', is the motto of which small English county that is home to one of the largest reservoirs in Western Europe?

    b.   Associated with the engineer noted for his work in draining the Fens, the motto of South Cambridgeshire District Council translates as 'nothing without effort', and is thought to be the only British civic motto in which language?

    c.   The city of Exeter and the town of Saint Malo in Brittany share what Latin motto, meaning 'always faithful'?

18 Give me both of the following terms used in physics, which differ by a single letter. One refers to a process or medium that is not dependent on direction; the other means 'pertaining to versions of an atom or nucleus that contain different numbers of neutrons'.

Three bonus questions on thermometers

a. Which English scientist gives his name to the first successful modern maximum-minimum thermometer, demonstrated in 1782?

b. The constant volume gas thermometer is used to calibrate other thermometers from which standard reference temperature, given the value of 273.16 Kelvin?

c. Resistance thermometers are temperature sensors based on predictable changes in electrical resistance, almost all of them being made of which metal?

19 Born in 1905, which Dutch-born astronomer found carbon dioxide in the atmosphere of Mars, discovered the dense atmosphere of Saturn's moon Titan, and gave his name to a large belt of icy bodies orbiting beyond Neptune?

Three bonus questions on animals and constellations

a. The constellation Aquila and its brightest star Altair are named, in Latin and Arabic respectively, after which bird? It appears in Greek mythology as the carrier of Zeus's thunderbolt.

b. Said to represent the dove released from the Ark by Noah, which constellation shares its name with a sixth-century saint who established a monastery on the Hebridean island of Iona?

c. Volans is a small constellation in the southern hemisphere representing a fish of the family *Exocoetidae*, found in warm and tropical waters, characterised by enlarged pectoral fins, and known by what common name?

20 Familiar on UK high streets from the 1930s onwards, what word derived from the Greek meaning 'song' and originally meant a hall in which poets and musicians contended for prizes in ancient Greece and Rome?

Three bonus questions on the deaths of Roman emperors, according to Suetonius in his *Lives of the Caesars*

a. The death of which emperor in AD 68 provoked, according to Suetonius, 'such great public joy that the common people ran through the city dressed in liberty caps'?

b. Dying at the age of 63 in AD 54, which emperor 'towards the end of his life gave some unambiguous indications that he regretted both his marriage to Agrippina and his adoption of Nero'?

c. On the day before he met his death in AD 41, aged 28, which emperor dreamt 'that he was standing in the heavens next to Jupiter's throne, and that Jupiter pushed him with the big toe of his right foot so that he fell headlong to Earth'?

21 In his 'picture theory of meaning', which philosopher expressed the view that a sentence must share a pictorial form with whatever state of affairs it reports? The theory appeared in the 1921 work *Tractatus Logico-Philosophicus*.

Three bonus questions on philosophy in the 1650s

a. Which work of 1651 is named after a sea monster mentioned in the Book of Job? The author uses its immense power as a metaphor for the power of the state he describes.

b. Which philosopher left the Jewish community in Amsterdam in 1656, possibly under pressure from the authorities because of his rationalist approach to religion? His best-known work is the posthumously published *Ethics*.

c. In the mid-1650s, which French philosopher wrote the anonymous *Provincial Letters*, attacking the casuistry of the Jesuits?

22 What given name links: a founder of the Cistercian order, born around 1028; the eldest son of William the Conqueror who succeeded him as Duke of Normandy; and three kings of Scotland, the first of whom was the victor at the Battle of Bannockburn in 1314?

Three bonus questions on geography

a. Argentina is the eighth-largest country in the world. Which landlocked Asian country is the ninth largest?

b. The two countries with an area closest to that of the United Kingdom are in Africa. The Republic of Guinea is a little larger. Which landlocked country in East Africa is slightly smaller?

c. Of the 28 EU member states, which has a total area closest to that of the UK?

23 Named after the Pyrenean town where they were discovered in 1904, the 'Homilies of Organya' date to the late thirteenth century and are one of the earliest texts of which romance language?

Three bonus questions on circumlocutions of the US military

a. What piece of equipment, often used by soldiers on manoeuvres, was given the name 'frame-supported tension structure' by the Pentagon?

b. On one occasion, 'hexaform rotatable surface compression unit' was the Pentagon's term for which object?

c. What is the usual English word for what the Pentagon has called an 'aerodynamic personnel decelerator'?

24 Listen carefully. Names denoting the current geological era, the President of France from 1995 to 2007, and the writing system used in Bulgarian and Russian all begin and end with which letter of the alphabet?

Three bonus questions on an actor

a. *Trouble in Store*, *The Square Peg* and *The Bulldog Breed* were among the films of which comedian and actor, who died, aged 90, in 2010?

b. Possibly as a result of information inserted in Wikipedia, several national newspapers erroneously stated that Norman Wisdom wrote the lyrics of which 1941 song, made famous by Vera Lynn?

c. Norman Wisdom was one of the few western actors whose films were permitted to be shown in which country during the dictatorship of Enver Hoxha?

25 In 1961, who became the first living artist to have his work exhibited at the Louvre? His paintings include *Terrace of Hotel Mistral*, *The Portuguese* and *Violin and Candlestick*.

Three bonus questions on cafés

a. Its former patrons including Camus and Picasso, which café on Saint-Germain-des-Prés in Paris takes its name from the two carved wooden statues of Chinese commercial agents which form part of the interior?

b. Which 1951 story by Carson McCullers tells of the tragedy of Miss Amelia, who opens an eating establishment in a small town in the American South?

c. Which Dutch artist painted *Night Café* in 1888, of which he wrote, 'I have tried to express with red and green the terrible passions of human nature'?

26 What seven-letter word denotes both Austria under Nazi rule and, informally, the currency of the former German Democratic Republic?

Three bonus questions on film noir screenplays

a. Which Anglo-American author of detective fiction wrote the screenplay for the 1946 film noir *The Blue Dahlia*, starring Veronica Lake?

b. Co-written by Chandler and Billy Wilder, which 1944 film noir starred Barbara Stanwyck, was based on a novel by James Cain, and took its title from a term used in life insurance policies?

c. Chandler also collaborated on the screenplay of which 1951 film, directed by Alfred Hitchcock and based on a novel by Patricia Highsmith about a proposed double murder?

27 Later identified with King Arthur, which battle of the early sixth century was described by the chronicler Gildas as having given the British several decades of respite against the invading Saxons? Its site is unknown, but is thought by some to be Liddington Castle, near Badbury in Wiltshire.

Three bonus questions on homonyms, words with a shared pronunciation but different meanings or spellings. For each of the following pairs, spell both words, in the order of the definitions given.

a. A strip of cloth wound round the lower leg and formerly worn by soldiers, and a cement made from chalk and linseed oil used for fixing glass in frames?

b. To become wearisome through familiarity, and a curved bar whose free end engages with a cogwheel to ensure movement in only one direction?

c. A feeling of anger or resentment resulting from a slight or injury, especially to one's pride, and the summit of a mountain?

28 To which nearby island in the Venetian Lagoon were the glassmaking factories of Venice transferred at the end of the thirteenth century, remaining there to the present day?

Three bonus questions on Italian artists

a. What was the surname of the Venetian Renaissance artists Jacopo and his sons, Gentile and Giovanni? The latter's works include *The Agony in the Garden* in the National Gallery.

b. Bellini's *The Agony in the Garden* is thought to have been influenced by a painting of the same name, also in the National Gallery, by which artist, who was also Bellini's brother-in-law?

c. Gentile Bellini is noted for a portrait, now in the National Gallery, of the ruler of which state, at whose court he worked from 1479 to 1481?

29 Which two final letters link words meaning: an arrangement of five things, as on a playing card; the upper part of the windpipe; the language of the Isle of Man; and a monster with the head of a woman and the body of a lioness?

Three bonus questions on words that contain all five vowels, in any order. In each case, give the word from the description.

    a. A cultivar of *Brassica oleracea*, whose varieties include Snowball, Clapton and Romanesco Veronica?

    b. An adjective describing something that is beyond one's reach, or that cannot be acquired or procured by effort?

    c. A small percussion instrument, appearing in the title of a song written and recorded by Bob Dylan and covered by The Byrds?

30 In chemistry, what seven-letter adjective is used to describe non-systematic names such as 'chloroform' for trichloromethane, and 'carbolic acid' for hydroxybenzene? In everyday speech, the same word means 'paltry' or 'of small account'.

Three bonus questions on the vertebrate ear

    a. In tetrapods, what term denotes the canal connecting the pharynx with the middle ear? It permits equalisation of pressure on either side of the tympanic membrane.

    b. The vestibular and cochlear nerves are branches of the cranial nerve denoted by what number?

    c. Which ossicle is attached to the tympanic membrane?

The Answers

1 Les Six / The Six
- **a.** *Futurama*
- **b.** Monty Python('s Flying Circus; precise titles vary between records, stage versions, etc.)
- **c.** *The Big Bang Theory*

2 Yuccas
- **a.** Envy
- **b.** Sloth
- **c.** Lust

3 (John) Keats (the first line of *Endymion*)
- **a.** Hydrogen
- **b.** Xenon
- **c.** Helium

4 'U' and 'i' (Uighurs, Uitlander, Uist – South and North)
- **a.** *Finnegans Wake*
- **b.** A gull's (or bird's) cry (or caw or squawk, etc.)
- **c.** Monomyth

5 Eke
- **a.** Steradian (12.566 being equal to 4 pi)
- **b.** 41,000 (41,253)
- **c.** Half a degree

6 (The Treaty of) Rome
- **a.** *(The) School for Scandal*

    b.   Zoë Heller

    c.   (John) Profumo

7 Lamarckism (Jean-Baptiste Lamarck)

    a.   (John Everett) Millais

    b.   (Edward White) Benson

    c.   William Booth

8 Rococo (Fr: rocaille; It: barocco)

    a.   Lithosphere

    b.   Asthenosphere

    c.   Plate tectonics (accept continental drift; his 1915 paper 'Origin of Continents and Oceans' concerned continental drift. The mechanism of plate tectonics was not introduced until 1929 by Arthur Holmes, but allow either answer)

9 38 (xxxviii)

    a.   Chiang Kai-Shek

    b.   Sun Yat-Sen / Sun Zhongshan

    c.   Finance minister

10 (Thomas) Malthus (Rev. Thomas Robert Malthus, 1766–1834)

    a.   (John T.) Scopes / the Scopes Trial

    b.   Martin Guerre (the imposter Arnaud du Tilh claimed to be the missing Guerre, and lived with Guerre's wife, until the real Guerre returned)

    c.   (Stephenson's) *Rocket*

11 Short (Short Parliament / shorthand / short circuit)

    a.   Enormous (Latin: *enormis*, 'unusual')

    b.   Immense ('im' + 'mensus')

    c.   Gargantuan (from Rabelais, *The Life of Gargantua and Pantagruel*)

12 *Decapoda* / decapods

a.   (Leonid) Brezhnev
b.   Frank Sinatra doctrine (i.e. that Warsaw Pact countries could do socialism 'their way')
c.   Truman doctrine (in 1947)

13 Antibiotic / anti-bacterial / anti-microbial
a.   Parenchyma
b.   Meristem (Greek: *merizein*, 'divide into two')
c.   Cambium

14 Odd integers (when *n* is odd)
a.   Jenny Saville
b.   Gillian Wearing
c.   Sam Taylor-Wood

15 16.1 per cent (so accept 14 per cent–18.1 per cent)
a.   Axel
b.   Salchow
c.   Lutz

16 (Queen) Mab
a.   *Julius Caesar*
b.   *Henry the Sixth, Part Three* (must include 'Part Three')
c.   Aristotle

17 Thomas Hardy
a.   Rutland
b.   Dutch (Cornelius Vermuyden, 1595–1677, brought Dutch drainage techniques to the UK)
c.   Semper fidelis

18 Isotropic, isotopic (accept isotrope, isotope)
a.   (James) Six (Six's Thermometer)
b.   The triple point of water
c.   Platinum

19 (Gerard) Kuiper (1905–1973; NB not Oort – the Oort Belt is hypothetical and more distant, and Oort was born in 1900; not Van Allen – the Van Allen belt is a radiation belt around the Earth, and Van Allen was US-born)
- **a.** Eagle
- **b.** Columba (Latin for 'dove'; identified by Dutch astronomer Petrus Plancius in 1592 and named by him Columba Noachi, 'Noah's Dove')
- **c.** Flying fish (the constellation was originally named Piscis Volans)

20 Odeon (from the Greek 'ode')
- **a.** Nero
- **b.** Claudius
- **c.** Caligula

21 (Ludwig) Wittgenstein
- **a.** *Leviathan* (Thomas Hobbes)
- **b.** (Baruch) Spinoza
- **c.** (Blaise) Pascal

22 Robert (Saint Robert of Molesme; Robert Curthose; Robert the Bruce)
- **a.** Kazakhstan
- **b.** Uganda (much larger: Kenya, Tanzania, Ethiopia, Mozambique; much smaller: Rwanda, Burundi, Malawi)
- **c.** Romania (UK, 242,900 square kilometres; Romania, 238,391 square kilometres; Italy and Poland are both considerably bigger)

23 Catalan
- **a.** Tent
- **b.** Nut
- **c.** Parachute

24 'C' (Cenozoic, Chirac, Cyrillic)
- **a.** Norman Wisdom

b. '(There'll Be Bluebirds Over) The White Cliffs of Dover'

c. Albania

25 (Georges) Braque (1882–1963; NB Matisse was dead by then – he died in 1954)

    a. Les Deux Magots (a magot being a carved, often grotesque figurine of East Asian origin)

    b. *The Ballad of the Sad Café*

    c. (Vincent) van Gogh

26 Ostmark

    a. Raymond Chandler

    b. *Double Indemnity*

    c. *Strangers on a Train*

27 (Mount) Badon / Mons Badonicus

    a. Puttee / putty

    b. Pall / pawl

    c. Pique / peak

28 Murano (fear of fire was the main reason for their removal from Venice)

    a. Bellini

    b. (Andrea) Mantegna

    c. The Ottoman Empire (Mehmet the Second)

29 '-nx' (quincunx, larynx, Manx, sphinx)

    a. Cauliflower

    b. Unobtainable

    c. Tambourine ('Mr Tambourine Man')

30 Trivial

    a. Eustachian tube (or canal; accept auditory or pharyngo-tympanic tube)

    b. 8 (eighth)

    c. Malleus (allow hammer; the other ossicles are the incus and the stapes)

Match Five

1 Answer as soon as you buzz. The names of two US states end in a letter 's' that is not pronounced as an 's'. For ten points, name both states.

Three bonus questions on layers of the atmosphere

a. The name of which layer of the atmosphere means, in part, 'turning'? It is marked by convection and a general decrease of temperature with height.

b. The ionosphere lies primarily within which layer of the atmosphere? It begins at about 85 kilometres, and within it the temperature can rise to over one thousand degrees Celsius.

c. What name is given to the layer that is situated above the stratosphere and is separated from it by the stratopause?

2 Produced in bone marrow and found in the blood of all mammals, which small disc-like structures are important factors in stopping bleeding and in healing wounds?

Three bonus questions on property

a. 'Government has no other end but the preservation of property.' Who wrote these words in his *Second Treatise on Civil Government* of 1690?

b. 'Property and law are born together, and die together. Before the laws, there was no property: take away laws, and property ceases.' Which English philosopher wrote these words in *Principles of the Civil Code*?

c. 'In no country of the world is the love of property more active and more anxious than in the United States.' Which Frenchman wrote these words in a work of 1835 entitled *Democracy in America*?

3 From that of a marshal of France, what name was originally given to a confection made by browning almonds or other nuts in boiling sugar, but now usually refers to a smooth paste made from this, often used as a filling in chocolates?

Three bonus questions on place names

a. Around the size of the Isle of Mull and at a latitude of 38 degrees north, Sado is the sixth-largest island of which country?

b. Reaching the Atlantic Ocean near the city of Setubal, the Sado is a major river of which country?

c. The village of Sadová in the Czech Republic gives its name to the decisive battle of which war of 1866?

4 Which year saw the publication of Einstein's first paper, on capillarity; the eleventh United Kingdom census; the births of Barbara Cartland and Louis Armstrong, and the deaths of President William McKinley and Queen Victoria?

Three bonus questions on fishing in literature

a. Which US author's collection of writings on fishing, published posthumously in 2000, include his experiences of the sport in Paris, the Pyrenees, Spain and Cuba?

b. *Trout Fishing in America* and *A Confederate General from Big Sur* are works by which US novelist and poet, who died in 1984?

c. Along with 'Salmon Fishing', the name of which country of the Middle East appears in the title of a prizewinning first novel by Paul Torday?

5 'If a man love the labour of any trade, apart from any question of success or fame, the gods have called him.' These words appear in *Across the Plains*, a travel memoir of 1892 by which literary figure? Best known for his adventure novels, he was born in Edinburgh and died in Samoa.

Three bonus questions on writers' private lives

a. Henrietta Godolphin, the second Duchess of Marlborough, was the lover of which playwright? He is believed to have fathered her child Mary in 1723, and was also known to be close to the actress Anne Bracegirdle, for whom he wrote parts in several of his works.

b. Quote: 'Remember thee! Remember thee! / Till Lethe quench life's burning stream / Remorse and shame shall cling to thee, / And haunt thee like a feverish dream!' Which Romantic poet wrote these lines as a rejection of the repeated advances of his former lover?

c. Who, between 1660 and 1669, chronicled his affairs with William Bagwell's wife; Jane Welsh, the servant of his barber; Sarah from the Swan inn; Betty Martin; and Deb Willet, the latter being his own wife's maidservant?

6 What part of the body appears in nicknames given to 'Peace Democrats' in the North during the American Civil War, and supporters of Parliament during the English Civil War?

Three bonus questions on comparative religion

a. 'Religion is hard work. Its insights are not self-evident and have to be cultivated in the same way as an appreciation of art, music, or poetry must be developed.' These are the words of which British author, in the 2009 work *The Case for God*?

b. An examination of thought between 900 and 200 BC, Karen Armstrong's work *The Great Transformation* includes the names of four influential figures in its subtitle. One is Jeremiah. For five points, name two of the others.

c. A 2010 work by Armstrong outlines twelve steps to a life based on what quality, described as 'indispensable to the creation of a just economy and a peaceful global community'?

7 A large public square flanked by Islamic academies, the Registan is a UNESCO world heritage site in which Central Asian city? Known as Maracanda when it was captured by Alexander the Great, it later became Tamerlane's capital and is today in Uzbekistan.

Three bonus questions on education in the United States

a. Having a different meaning in the UK, what name is given to American secondary schools, usually independent, that educate students up to college entrance level?

b. What term denotes a type of secondary school in the UK, and in the USA means a primary school or a school stressing the study of classical languages?

c. Sometimes called 'grammar' or 'elementary' schools, American primary schools are also known by what name, not used in the UK?

8 For what do the letters f.p.s. stand when denoting a system of units for length, mass and time that has been superseded for scientific purposes by the SI system?

Three bonus questions on dates in novels

a. In which novel of 1895 does an inventor encounter people called the Eloi and the Morlocks in the year 802,701?

b. Aldous Huxley's novel *Brave New World* is set in the year 632 AF; for what do the letters 'AF' stand?

c. In which novel of 1889 by Mark Twain does a contemporary American experience life in the year 528?

9 *Dead Christ* and *Dance of Death* were works by which German artist, who settled in England in 1532 and is also noted for his portraits, including those of Sir Thomas More and of Henry the Eighth and his wives?

Three bonus questions on Greek mythology

a. Eurycleia was the nurse of which hero, whom she recognised after many years by a scar on his leg made by a wild boar?

b. Against Odysseus's orders, the crewman Eurylochus persuades his fellows to slaughter cattle belonging to which deity? As a result, Zeus sends a storm that causes all but Odysseus to drown.

c. Both killed by Odysseus, Eurymachus and Antinous are the two principal suitors of which figure?

10 In quantum physics, which subatomic particle, a meson with a mass of about 9.4 gigaelectron-volts and a zero charge, is thought to consist of a b-quark and its anti-quark? It is named after the twentieth letter of the Greek alphabet.

Three bonus questions on exiles

a. Saint John is said to have written the Book of Revelation while in exile on which Greek island in the Aegean Sea?

b. Which Spanish painter and engraver, whose etchings *The Disasters of War* depicted the horrors of the French invasion of Spain, spent his last years in voluntary exile in Bordeaux?

c. In 1960, after leaving Tibet, at which hill station in northern India did the Dalai Lama set up his government in exile?

11 Who was the author of a manuscript over 200 years old which sold at Sotheby's in 2011 for almost a million pounds? An unfinished novel, it concerns a young woman who returns to her father's household after being brought up by a wealthy aunt, and is titled 'The Watsons'.

Three bonus questions on the novels of Ian McEwan. In each case, identify the novel from the description of its main character.

a. Henry Perowne, a 48-year-old neurosurgeon, in a novel described as 'a post 9/11 variation' on Virginia Woolf's *Mrs Dalloway*?

b. Michael Beard, a Nobel laureate devoted to womanising, inordinate consumption of food and drink, and the averting of climate change?

c. Briony Tallis, who at the start of the novel is 13 years old and writing a play for her brother, Leon?

12 A flat layer of carbon atoms tightly packed into a two-dimensional honeycomb arrangement, which material is both the thinnest and the strongest material known to science, and conducts electricity better than copper? Experiments with it led two Manchester University scientists to win the 2010 Nobel Prize for Physics.

Three bonus questions on pollination of flowers

a. Derived from the Greek meaning 'closed marriage', what term means a form of self-pollination within a permanently closed flower?

b. The pollen of many orchids is transferred as a single agglutinated mass. What name is given to this mass of pollen grains?

c. *The Various Contrivances by which Orchids Are Pollinated by Insects* is an 1862 work by which scientist?

13 Which monarch occupies the north east, if the south west is occupied by General Sir Charles James Napier, and the south east by Major General Sir Henry Havelock?

Three bonus questions on rivers of the Midlands

a. Which river rises on Biddulph Moor in Staffordshire and joins the Yorkshire Ouse after 45 miles to form the Humber? One of its crossings gives its name to a county cricket ground.

b. Which Midlands town and borough takes its name from the River Tame, which joins the River Anker there?

c. Which river flows through the West Midlands and bisects Kidderminster from north to south before joining the Severn at a river port to which it gives its name?

14 Similar to Spanish paella, which Creole dish has a Louisiana French name that is derived from the Provençal word for 'chicken and rice stew'?

Three bonus questions on pairs of words whose spelling differs by the substitution of a 'd' for an 'f' for the final letter, for example 'deaf' and 'dead'. In each case, give both words from the definitions.

a. 'Organ of photosynthesis in plants' and 'soft, grey metallic element, atomic number 82'?

b. 'Rocks or coral near the surface of water' and 'vibrating tongue of a woodwind instrument'?

c. 'Canis lupus' and 'open tract of upland country, for example in Lincolnshire'?

15 First published in 1957, Vance Packard's book *The Hidden Persuaders* explained the methods used by which industry in tailoring campaigns to exploit psychological vulnerabilities among consumers?

Three bonus questions on the Nobel Prize for Literature

a. Which Irish writer won the award in 1969, being commended by the judges for writing which, quote: 'rises ... like a *miserere* from all mankind, its muffled minor key sounding liberation to the oppressed, and comfort to those in need'?

b. Which writer was praised by the 2006 committee for making Istanbul 'an indispensable literary territory equal to Dostoevsky's St Petersburg, Joyce's Dublin or Proust's Paris'?

   c. On winning the 1982 prize, which Colombian writer in his Nobel lecture talked of 'a new and sweeping utopia of life ... where the races condemned to one hundred years of solitude will have, at last and forever, a second opportunity on Earth'?

16 Deriving from the Latin for 'bone', what term denotes the chapel in Sedlec in the Czech Republic and Rome's Santa Maria della Concezione, both of which serve as repositories for the bones of the dead?

Three bonus questions on British seafood

   a. The invention of which fish delicacy is credited to John Woodger of Seahouses in Northumberland, who accidentally discovered the process of manufacture in 1843?

   b. The Norfolk village of Stiffkey is noted for which bivalve molluscs? The shells get their distinctive blue tinge from the sea-beds they colonise.

   c. Partly named after a fishing village in Moray, which rich soup is made with chopped potatoes, milk and flaked smoked haddock?

17 Listen carefully. If a single self-replicating robot takes one year to produce ten copies of itself, all of which are activated on the same day, after how many years will the number of robots exceed one million?

Three bonus questions on large numbers in the 'short scale' terms now commonly used in the UK; in each case, give the exponent of ten in the following quantities.

   a. One billion?

   b. One billion billion?

    c. One billion raised to the power one billion?

18 Included by Linnaeus as a cephalopod in his *Systema Naturae*, what mythological beast is the subject of a poem by Tennyson and an apocalyptic novel of 1953 by John Wyndham?

Three bonus questions on sisters in literature

    a. Both performers in a song-and-dance variety act, the twin sisters Nora and Dora Chance are the central characters in *Wise Children*, the final novel of which English writer?

    b. The sisters Cassandra and Julia Corbett, the former an Oxford don, the latter a writer, appear in *The Game*, a novel of 1967 by which author, who won the Booker Prize in 1990 and is herself the sister of a novelist?

    c. What is the surname of the sisters Ursula and Gudrun, who first appear in D.H. Lawrence's novel *The Rainbow*, and are the central characters in *Women in Love*?

19 Meanings of what seven-letter word include an anatomical structure resembling a bird's beak; a type of camera used to produce animated films; and a platform for public speaking?

Three bonus questions on island states of the Indian Ocean. In each case, name both the country and the capital described.

    a. The Indian Ocean state whose capital is named after a paramour of Madame de Pompadour?

    b. The Indian Ocean state whose capital shares its name with the angel said to have revealed the 'golden plates' that became the source of the Book of Mormon?

    c. The island state whose capital shares its name with both an Australian state and the capital of British Columbia?

20 According to details on packaging, which common cleansing agent may contain ingredients including: aqua, hydrated silica, sodium bicarbonate, propylene glycol, penta-sodium triphosphate, tetra-sodium pyrophosphate, sodium lauryl sulphate, sodium saccharin and calcium peroxide?

Three bonus questions on a disease

    a. Scrofula, now an uncommon condition usually acquired by drinking infected milk, is a form of which disease?

    b. In the Middle Ages, scrofula was believed to be curable by the physical touch of a monarch, and was consequently known by what name?

    c. As a small child, Samuel Johnson was brought to London to be touched by which monarch, the last in Britain to practise the custom?

21 In Chinese medicine, what English word denotes each of a set of pathways in the human body along which vital energy is said to flow? It can also mean a circle of constant longitude passing through a given place on the Earth's surface and the terrestrial poles.

Three bonus questions on space telescopes. In each case, I want to know the name of the broad energy band of the electromagnetic spectrum that each telescope detects.

    a. The Chandra Observatory?

    b. The Fermi space telescope?

    c. The Spitzer space telescope?

22 In which German city was the business of the financier Mayer Amschel Rothschild originally based?

Three bonus questions on pairs of anagrams. In each case, give both words from the definitions.

   a. A large company of musicians, and a large thick-set quadruped used for heavy work?

   b. A landlocked African country, and a verb meaning 'to rule over'?

   c. An adolescent, and a verb meaning 'produce' or 'create', for example electricity?

23 *La Casa de los Espiritus* and *De Amor y de Sombra* are the Spanish titles of two novels by which Peruvian-born Chilean author, who fled to Venezuela after Pinochet's military coup in 1973?

Three bonus questions where the answer in each case is the name of a country which, with a different meaning or etymology, would be permissible in a game of Scrabble, for example, 'China'. Give the name of the country from the definition.

   a. A fine goatskin leather tanned with sumac and used, for example, in bookbinding?

   b. A light, horse-drawn two-wheeled vehicle in India?

   c. A glossy black varnish or lacquer?

24 Which six-letter acronym is applied to those alloys of iron made into strong permanent magnets by the addition usually of aluminium, nickel and cobalt? It is particularly associated with an early type of nuclear reactor.

Three bonus questions on acronyms

a. For major investigations, UK police forces began in 1986 to employ a Home Office system known by what possibly appropriate acronym?

b. Vicap, standing for Violent Criminal Apprehension Programme, was established in the mid-1980s by which organisation?

c. First established by the Los Angeles police department in 1968, for what does the acronym 'Swat' stand when denoting US paramilitary law-enforcement units?

25 *Baal, Man Equals Man, Mother Courage and Her Children* and *The Life of Galileo* are works by which playwright, born in Bavaria in 1898?

Three bonus questions on a Dutch scientist

a. Born in 1629, which Dutch scientist gives his name to the principle that all points of a wave front of light in a vacuum are new sources of wavelets that expand in every direction?

b. Launched in 1997, Cassini-Huygens is a space mission to which planet, the subject of many observations by Huygens, including the discovery of its largest moon?

c. Huygen's interest in the accurate measurement of time led him to the discovery of what device as a regulator of clocks, an idea first explored by Galileo?

26 First performed in 1824, which piece of music is, in Japan, traditionally played as part of New Year celebrations? A theme from its fourth movement has been adapted as the European anthem 'Ode to Joy'.

Three bonus questions on elements discovered in 1817

a. Experimenting on zinc compounds in 1817, the German chemist Friedrich Strohmeyer found an impurity in zinc carbonate that he identified as which new element, a toxic, silver-white, ductile metal?

b. Also credited with having devised the modern system of chemical symbols and formulae, which Swedish chemist discovered silicon, cerium, thorium and, in 1817, selenium?

c. Discovered by one of his students in 1817, which element was named by Berzelius from the Greek for 'stone'?

27 Which cricketer was the oldest man to score a test century, doing so in the 1928–1929 season? A Surrey and England player, he was the sport's most prolific batsman, scoring 197 first-class centuries.

Three bonus questions on a conjunction

a. 'Anthologised to weariness', according to its author, which poem of 1910 describes triumph and disaster as 'those two imposters', and encourages the reader to treat them 'just the same'?

b. The 1969 film *If*, depicting life in a British public school and culminating in an armed insurrection, was directed by which film critic-turned-director?

c. In the context of the cardiac pacemaker current, what word is denoted by the letter 'f' in the abbreviation I_f?

28 Examples including New Zealand, Tuvalu and Barbados, what precise two-word term denotes a sovereign state that has the Queen as its monarch?

Three bonus questions on the Napoleonic Wars

a. The Battle of Aboukir Bay, a decisive victory for Nelson over Napoleon's fleet in 1798, is more commonly named after which river, a branch of which opens into the bay?

b. 'The Battle of the Three Emperors', a victory for Napoleon against Austria and Russia in December 1805, is better known by what name, after a town in Moravia?

c. A significant defeat for Napoleon, 'the Battle of the Nations' in October 1813 is also known by what name, after a city in Saxony?

29 Which epic poem ends with these lines: 'The World was all before them, where to choose / Their place of rest, and Providence their guide / They hand in hand with wand'ring steps and slow / Through Eden took their solitary way'?

Three bonus questions on the works of Friedrich Schiller. In each case, identify the title character of the work described.

a. A trilogy of plays based on the life of a bohemian general, assassinated in 1634?

b. An historical play about the last days of an exiled queen who was executed in 1587?

c. The story of a legendary fourteenth-century freedom fighter; it was later adapted into an opera by Rossini?

30 Fully elaborating his Structuralist approach to culture in the 1962 work *The Savage Mind*, which Belgian-born anthropologist also analysed myth narratives in *The Raw and the Cooked*? He died in October 2009, having reached his hundredth birthday.

Three bonus questions on Middle Eastern cities

a. Esfahan and Tabriz are major cities in which Middle Eastern country?

b. Which historic city in eastern Kerman Province was devastated by an earthquake in December 2003?

c. Situated close to the borders of Afghanistan and Turkmenistan, what is Iran's second largest city?

The Answers

1 Arkansas, Illinois
    a.   Troposphere (do not accept mesosphere)
    b.   Thermosphere
    c.   Mesosphere

2 Platelets / thrombocytes
    a.   John Locke
    b.   (Jeremy) Bentham
    c.   (Alexis) de Tocqueville

3 Praline (Marshal du Plessis-Praslin, 1598–1675)
    a.   Japan
    b.   Portugal
    c.   Austro-Prussian / Austro-German War / Seven Weeks' War (the battle is also known as Königgrätz)

4 1901
    a.   (Ernest) Hemingway (*Hemingway on Fishing*)
    b.   (Richard Gary) Brautigan
    c.   Yemen (*Salmon Fishing in the Yemen*, 2006)

5 Robert Louis Stevenson (1850–1894)
    a.   (William) Congreve
    b.   Lord Byron (to Lady Caroline Lamb)
    c.   Samuel Pepys

6 Head (Copperheads and Roundheads)
    a.   Karen Armstrong

b. Buddha, Socrates, Confucius (*The Great Transformation: The World in the Time of Buddha, Socrates, Confucius and Jeremiah*)

c. Compassion (*Twelve Steps to a Compassionate Life*)

7 Samarkand
a. Preparatory school (accept prep school; not public school)
b. Grammar school
c. Grade school(s)

8 Foot-pound-second
a. *The Time Machine* (by H.G. Wells)
b. After Ford (632 years after Henry Ford first mass-produced the motor car)
c. *A Connecticut Yankee in King Arthur's Court* (early versions were called *A Yankee at the Court of King Arthur*)

9 (Hans) Holbein (the Younger)
a. Odysseus / Ulysses
b. Hyperion / Helios / Sun god
c. Penelope (if they answer his wife, press for her name)

10 Upsilon
a. Patmos
b. Goya (Francisco José de Goya y Lucientes, 1746–1828)
c. Dharamsala (specifically in the McLeod Ganj suburb of Dharamsala)

11 Jane Austen
a. *Saturday* (2005)
b. *Solar* (2010)
c. *Atonement* (2001)

12 Graphene

    a.   Cleistogamy (Greek: *kleistos*, 'closed'; *gamos*, 'marriage')
    b.   Pollinium, pollinia
    c.   (Charles) Darwin

13 King George the Fourth (plinths in Trafalgar Square, of course)
    a.   Trent (Trent Bridge)
    b.   Tamworth
    c.   Stour (joins the Severn at Stourport-on-Severn)

14 Jambalaya (Provençal: *jambalaia*)
    a.   Leaf and lead
    b.   Reef and reed
    c.   Wolf and wold

15 Advertising
    a.   Samuel Beckett
    b.   Orhan Pamuk
    c.   Gabriel García Márquez

16 Ossuary (Latin: *oss*, 'bone')
    a.   Kippers / kippered herring
    b.   Cockles
    c.   Cullen skink (Cullen is the village)

17 Six years (i.e. 10 after 1 year, 100 after 2, 1,000 after 3, 10,000 after 4, 100,000 after 5, 1,000,000 after 6)
    a.   Nine (10 to the 9; not 12, and not 10 to the 12, which is the 'long-scale' one million million; 'short scale' denotes one thousand million)
    b.   Eighteen (10 to the 18)
    c.   Nine billion

18 The Kraken
    a.   Angela Carter
    b.   A.S. Byatt
    c.   Brangwen

19 Rostrum
- **a.** Mauritius, Port Louis (after Louis XV)
- **b.** Comoros, Moroni
- **c.** Seychelles, Victoria

20 Toothpaste (copied from a Colgate toothpaste packet)
- **a.** (Bovine) Tuberculosis
- **b.** (The) King's Evil (accept Queen's Evil)
- **c.** (Queen) Anne (in around 1711 or 1712)

21 Meridian
- **a.** X-ray(s)
- **b.** Gamma rays
- **c.** Infrared

22 Frankfurt (am Main)
- **a.** Orchestra and carthorse
- **b.** Niger and reign
- **c.** Teenager and generate

23 Isabel Allende
- **a.** Morocco
- **b.** Tonga
- **c.** Japan

24 Alnico (not the various trade names: Alcomax, Alni, Columax, Lycomax, Lodex, Ticonal, etc.)
- **a.** Holmes (Home Office Large Major Enquiry System, now superseded by Holmes 2)
- **b.** The FBI / Federal Bureau of Investigation
- **c.** Special Weapons And Tactics

25 (Bertolt) Brecht
- **a.** (Christiaan) Huygens (Huygens' principle)
- **b.** Saturn (Huygens discovered Titan in 1655)
- **c.** Pendulum

㉖ Beethoven's Ninth Symphony / Choral Symphony
    a.   Cadmium
    b.   (Jöns) Berzelius
    c.   Lithium

㉗ (Jack) Hobbs (Sir John Berry Hobbs, 1882–1963)
    a.   'If' (by Rudyard Kipling, of course)
    b.   Lindsay Anderson
    c.   Funny (funny current or funny channel, the pacemaker current)

㉘ Commonwealth Realm
    a.   The (Battle of the) Nile
    b.   Austerlitz
    c.   (The Battle of) Leipzig

㉙ *Paradise Lost* (by John Milton, of course)
    a.   Wallenstein (Albrecht von Wallenstein; the plays are *Wallenstein's Camp*, *The Piccolomini* and *Wallenstein's Death*)
    b.   Maria Stuart (accept Mary, Queen of Scots)
    c.   Wilhelm Tell / William Tell

㉚ (Claude) Lévi-Strauss
    a.   Iran
    b.   Bam
    c.   Mashhad

Match Six

1. Often seen as the grand finale of the cycling season, the Giro di Lombardia is a one-day race that has its finish at which lake, the third largest in Italy after Garda and Maggiore?

   Three bonus questions on the analysis of colour

   a. What component of HSI colour space is defined as the angle from red?

   b. What is the SI unit of luminous intensity?

   c. In the Cartesian RGB system, what would be seen if red, green and blue were of equal value and at their maxima?

2. Founded in 1675, which scientific research institution moved to Herstmonceux Castle in East Sussex in 1957 before moving to Cambridge in 1990?

   Three bonus questions on garden birds. In each case, give the common name of the bird from the binomial and the description of its call.

   a. *Parsus major*, whose distinctive two-syllable song has been compared to the phrase 'teacher teacher' repeated at high speed, or to the sound of a bicycle pump?

   b. *Prunella modularis*, whose call is a shrill and persistent 'tseep' while its song is a high-pitched bubbling sometimes likened to a squeaking trolley wheel?

    c. *Fringilla coelebs*, whose alarm call is an insistent 'pink pink' sound. Its song sounds like the phrase 'chip chip chip chooee chooee cheeoo'?

3 Meaning 'self-reliance', Juche is the national ideology promoted by the ruling regime of which Asian country? The words 'Democratic People's Republic' appear in its official name.

Three bonus questions on economics

    a. Frictional, structural and classical, the latter caused by excessively high wages, are three distinct types of what economic problem?

    b. Which law takes its name from the US economist who discovered that a one per cent increase in the unemployment rate, when above four per cent, was associated with a three per cent drop in the ratio of actual GNP to potential GNP?

    c. Named after an economist born in 1883, what type of unemployment results from insufficient aggregate demand in the economy to support all those who want to work?

4 Meanings of what two-letter word include: the twelfth star of a constellation; a temperate phage infecting various enterobacteria; a state of 'non being' or 'nothingness' in Zen Buddhism, and the Greek letter that is the symbol for a micron?

Three bonus questions on a constructed language

    a. Toki Pona is an experimental language first published online in 2001 by the Canadian linguist Sonja Elen Kisa. The word 'toki' means 'talk'; what is the meaning of 'pona', derived, via Esperanto, from Latin? Note that Toki Pona has no letter 'b'.

b. Toki Pona is intended to test the hypothesis that the words and forms of a language influence the way its users perceive the world. Which two linguists give their names to this hypothesis?

c. In Toki Pona, the word 'yo' means 'have', 'kon' means 'air', 'breath' means 'spirit' and 'sin' means 'new', and all derive from which major world language?

5 Born in 1905, which Dutch-American scientist gives his name to the region of the Solar System that stretches from the orbit of Neptune to an orbit approximately 55 astronomical units from the Sun?

Three bonus questions on multitasking

a. Which character in Gilbert and Sullivan's *The Mikado* holds numerous exalted offices, including Archbishop of Titipu, First Lord of the Treasury, and Lord High-Everything-Else?

b. In his capacity as Lord Chief Justice, Pooh-Bah sings the song 'I Am So Proud'. This includes which alliterative three-word phrase, now used to describe the way in which a judicial punishment might be experienced?

c. Claiming to be ignorant of the character, which Labour politician was, in December 2009, compared to Pooh-Bah because of the numerous Cabinet roles he held at the time?

6 Quote: 'His preoccupations with moral dilemma and his persistent choice of locations that were "seedy" – a word he was to regret popularising – give his work a highly distinctive quality.' These words refer to which novelist, whose best-known early work is the 1932 *Stamboul Train*?

Three bonus questions on shipping firsts

a. Launched in 1859, the French ship *La Gloire* was the first of what type of oceangoing warship? It was followed by the British HMS *Warrior* a year later.

b. The Soviet naval icebreaker *Lenin*, launched in 1957, was the first surface ship to be powered by what means?

c. In the early 1900s, Enrico Forlanini built the first of what type of vessel which, when moving, is lifted out of the water by a flat or curved fin-like device, attached by struts to the hull?

7 Including the Hox genes, what class of genes plays a central role in controlling the early patterns of development and differentiation of embryonic tissues? Mutation in these genes may cause growth in an inappropriate place, for example a foot instead of an antenna in a fly.

Three bonus questions on an African country

a. Which African country encloses Gambia on three sides and shares its name with the river that runs along its northern border?

b. Dakar, the capital of Senegal, is situated at the tip of which peninsula, the westernmost point of Africa?

c. Prior to independence in 1960, Senegal formed a short-lived federation with French Sudan. By what name is the latter country now known?

8 Listen carefully. For what real values of x and y does the square of x plus y equal x-squared plus y-squared?

Three bonus questions on mathematics. Name each of the following well-known conjectures, only the second of which has been resolved.

a. There are infinitely many prime numbers p, such that p plus two is also prime.

b. Does there exist an algorithm to determine whether an arbitrary polynomial Diophantine equation with integer coefficients has an integer solution?

c. Every even number greater than two is a sum of two primes?

9 What short word can follow 'Canopic', 'Mason', 'Kilner', 'killing' and 'Leyden' to describe specific types of container?

Three bonus questions on shared surnames

a. What surname was shared by a niece and uncle, the former a fashion designer associated with the colour 'shocking pink', the latter an astronomer whose observations of markings on the surface of Mars led to speculation about life on the planet?

b. What name links: the composer of the operas *Norma* and *La Sonnambula*, a Venetian painter known for his altarpieces, and an anatomist who described the excretory ducts of the kidney now named after him?

c. Which London-born clown, who died in 1837, shares his surname with the Genoese family who became lords of Monaco in the late thirteenth century?

10 Admirers of which author hold an annual 'Bloomsday' celebration on 16 June in honour of one of his novels, the action of which takes place on that day in 1904?

Three bonus questions on a novel

a. Give the author and the work of 1961 in which the following words appear: 'One's prime is elusive. You little girls, when you grow up, must be on the alert to recognise your prime at whatever time of your life it may occur.'

b. In the novel, Spark writes that Miss Brodie's pupils 'knew the rudiments of astrology but not the date of the Battle of Flodden or the capital of Finland'. So, for five points, give me both the date of the Battle of Flodden and the capital of Finland.

c. Give the four words that complete these lines that Miss Brodie recited to her class 'to raise their minds before they went home': 'Down she came and found a boat / Beneath a willow left afloat, / And round about the prow she wrote...' what?

11 Of the 118 elements of the periodic table, two have symbols which, when read as ordinary English words, become personal pronouns. One is iodine. Name the other.

Three bonus questions on pharmacology

a. Anti-pyretic pharmaceuticals serve to reduce what general medical condition?

b. What is reduced by the group of pharmaceuticals known as sartans?

c. What lipid component of plasma is lowered by the class of drug known as statins?

12 What French term denotes a feature formed by the erosion of ice in glaciated regions which takes the form of a bowl-shaped, steep-sided hollow at the head of a mountain valley?

Three bonus questions on French writers' pseudonyms

a. What pseudonym was adopted by Marie-Henri Beyle, reputedly after the similar name of the German town which was the birthplace of the archaeologist and art critic Johann Winckelmann?

b. Which writer's first works were published under the pseudonym 'Willy', the nickname of her first husband Henri Gauthier-Villars, although she later wrote under her own maiden surname?

c. Thought to have been taken from a village of the same name in the Midi, the dramatist Jean-Baptiste Poquelin adopted what name in the 1640s?

13 Which pioneer of the High Renaissance style designed part of Milan's Church of Santa Maria delle Grazie early in his career, and in 1503 became the chief architect of St Peter's Basilica in Rome?

Three bonus questions on English town halls

a. A statue of which Anglo-Saxon noblewoman stands beneath the central gable of the council house of the city of Coventry?

b. The subject of a biography by the historian Tacitus, a statue of which Roman general stands above the doorway of Manchester Town Hall?

c. Symbolising the city's traditional industries, a statue of which Roman god stands on top of Sheffield Town Hall?

14 From the Latin meaning 'to shear', what term denotes the shaving of the crown of the head in the Roman Catholic church before 1972 on admission to the priesthood or a monastic order?

Three bonus questions on translations of the Bible

a. Often abbreviated to LXX, what title is given to the earliest surviving Greek translation of the Hebrew Bible, and refers to the belief that seventy-two translators produced identical versions in seventy-two days?

b. The first printed edition of a complete English Bible, published in 1535, was translated by which reformer, after whom it is usually named?

c. The 'Treacle Bible' of 1568 is so called because Jeremiah 8:22 reads 'Is there no treacle in Gilead'; what word takes the place of 'treacle' in the Authorised Version?

15 13 July 2010 was the twenty-fifth anniversary of what event, ultimately prompted by the BBC news report in 1984 on Claire Bertschinger's work at a Red Cross feeding centre in northern Ethiopia?

Three bonus questions on self

a. *The Divided Self: An Existential Study in Sanity and Madness* is a 1960 work by which Scottish psychiatrist, also noted for *The Politics of Experience*?

b. Which novel by Will Self describes a future society in which the misogynistic rantings of an eponymous twentieth-century London taxi driver, printed on steel, are treated as revealed truth?

c. A former public prosecutor under the Nazis, Gerhard Self is an elderly private investigator in works by which German novelist, also noted for *The Reader*?

16 In physics, what term describes the process of varying an electromagnetic wave or other oscillating signal, especially in order to impress a signal on it? It is usually preceded by a noun such as 'frequency' or 'pulse'.

Three bonus questions on scientific terms, specifically, those that can be made from the eight letters of the word 'coxswain'. In each case, give the word from the description.

a. A long, threadlike part of a nerve cell that transmits impulses from the cell body?

b. The adjectival form of a medical term meaning a deficient supply of oxygen to the tissues?

c. An imaginary line about which a body rotates?

17 Quote: 'Here is something more terrible than Cain killing Abel; it is Washington killing Spartacus.' These words of Victor Hugo refer to the execution of which US abolitionist after an attack on a federal arsenal at Harper's Ferry in Virginia in 1859?

Three bonus questions on ballet dancers

a. Which Cuban dancer joined the Royal Ballet, Covent Garden in 1998, and was the first Westerner to dance the title role of *Spartacus* with the Bolshoi Ballet?

b. Margot Fonteyn declared which Australian dancer to be her favourite partner? In addition to his many classical ballet roles, he made a memorable appearance as the Child Catcher in the film version of *Chitty Chitty Bang Bang*.

c. Born in Kiev in about 1890, which dancer and choreographer was famed for his extraordinary elevation? He retired at the age of 29 after suffering a nervous breakdown.

18 Answer as soon as you buzz. Charles Dickens wrote six full-length novels with titles that do not include a character's name. *A Tale of Two Cities* is one. For ten points, name three of the others.

Three bonus questions on the Pulitzer Prize

a. Which political figure won the 1957 prize in biography for *Profiles in Courage*, recounting acts of bravery and integrity by US senators?

b. Which trumpeter became the first jazz artist to win the prize for music when he won the award for his 1997 performance piece 'Blood on the Fields'?

c. In April 2010, the *Newstoons* cartoonist Mark Fiore became the first journalist to win a Pulitzer while working solely in what medium?

19 'Memorable as the most characteristic incarnation of the secular spirit of the Papacy of the fifteenth century.' These words from the 1902 *Encyclopedia Britannica* refer to which figure, born in 1431? I'll accept his given name and surname, or his regnal name and number as Pontiff.

Three bonus questions on a theologian

a. Born in 1033 and often regarded as the founder of scholasticism, which Benedictine monk expounded the ontological proof for the existence of God in his *Proslogion*?

b. Anselm was enthroned as Archbishop of Canterbury during the reign of which king, who had kept the See vacant for several years to exploit its revenues?

c. In 1720, Pope Clement the Eleventh bestowed what title on Anselm, shared, among others, by Saint Augustine and Pope Gregory the First and acknowledging the significance of his writing to the Catholic Church as a whole?

20 Now the eastern part of Hiroshima prefecture, which former province of Japan shares its name with that of a popular British gambling game, the name often being used to express sudden success?

Three bonus questions on the arts

a. First performed in 1782, which Mozart opera is set in the Ottoman Empire?

b. Set in the final years of the Ottoman Empire, the 2004 novel *Birds Without Wings* is the work of which author?

c. The Ottoman Empire is the setting for the latter part of which 1981 film, directed by Peter Weir and starring Mel Gibson?

21 Between 1929 and 1938, which Essex rectory became the subject of a controversial series of 'ghost hunts' conducted by the paranormal investigator Harry Price? In 1940, after the building had burned down, he published his research under the title *The Most Haunted House in England*.

Three bonus questions on printers' marks

a. What word, meaning a stone pillar with a pointed top, is the alternative name for the typographical sign called a 'dagger', used for footnotes or other references?

b. The typographical mark called a 'pilcrow', resembling a reversed and in-filled capital letter 'P', is a familiar ASCII character on a computer screen indicating what?

c. What word or term is abbreviated by the symbol often found in legal documents approximately resembling a double letter 's'?

22 Give the precise two-word description of the region of the world specified by President Eisenhower in a speech of January 1957 in which he outlined a 'doctrine' that offered economic and military support for the containment of Soviet influence?

Three bonus questions on a civilisation

a. Uaxactun and Copan were principal cities of which civilisation, which flourished from around AD 250 to 900?

b. Abandoned in about the year 900 for reasons which are not fully understood, the Maya ceremonial centre of Tikal lies in which present-day country?

c. A fundamental part of the Mayan calendar was the period of 584 days, derived from the observation of a complete cycle of which planet?

23 A concordance of Shakespeare's plays reveals that the word 'melt' appears most frequently in which play, as in the lines: 'The crown o' the earth doth melt', and 'Let Rome in Tiber melt'?

Three bonus questions on melting points

a. Name the two elements which are liquid at 20 degrees Celsius, one having the atomic number 80, the other having an atomic mass of approximately 80?

b. Which Group One element is solid at normal human body temperature, but melts at a fever temperature of 39.31 degrees Celsius?

c. What is the only element that, in pure form and at standard atmospheric pressure, can remain solid above 3,500 degrees Celcius?

Probably founded by James the Third of Scotland in the fifteenth century, which order of knighthood was revived by James the Seventh and Second in 1687? It comprises the sovereign and sixteen knights and its motto is Nemo me impune lacessit, or 'No one provokes me with impunity'.

Three bonus questions on words; specifically, new definitions recently added to existing words in the online Oxford English Dictionary

a. 'A style of collarless neckline that closes with a short row of buttons or press studs' was added to which headword, also defined as 'a town on the Thames in Oxfordshire'?

b. 'Designating debt which has a high risk of default' was added to the meanings of what word, initially defined as 'of the nature of a poison'?

c. What word meaning engrained dirt was given this extra definition: 'A genre of popular music originating in East London, characterized by a minimal, prominent rhythm, a very low-pitched bassline, and vocals by an M.C.'?

25 The first was created in London in 1864, the second in Paris in 1889 and the third, founded by Lenin, was abolished in 1943; what name denotes these attempts at co-operative organisations of socialist, communist and revolutionary groups?

Three bonus questions on Marilyn Monroe

a. Marilyn Monroe's character in the 1953 film *Gentleman Prefer Blondes* shares her first name with which siren of German folklore, who lured men to their death in the River Rhine?

b. In which 1955 film, directed by Billy Wilder and also starring Tom Ewell, is Marilyn Monroe simply credited as 'The Girl'?

c. The Broadway musical *Sugar* took its title from the name of Monroe's character in which film, on which the musical was based?

26 In the following approximations, how many zeros follow the number given if the Earth's circumference in metres is 40, the number of seconds in a year is 31 and the number of identified insect species is 'one'?

Three bonus questions on acids

a. Muriatic acid and 'spirits of salts' are names formerly given to which highly corrosive mineral acid?

b. Nitric acid, the chemical usually combined with hydrochloric acid to form aqua regis, used to dissolve gold, was formerly known by what alchemical name?

c. Oil of vitriol is an earlier name for the concentrated form of which acid?

27 The name of which type of popular cuisine begins place names denoting a region of the Karakoram mountains, the largest city of Maryland, and a sea of northern Europe that is almost landlocked?

Three bonus questions on Pacific islands

a. Around the size of Wales, Grande Terre is the main island of which French collectivity? Situated 1,500 kilometres east of Queensland, Captain Cook is said to have named it after his father's homeland.

b. A little less than half the size of Scotland, the island of New Britain is part of which Pacific island state?

c. Before independence in 1980, which Pacific island state was known as the condominium of the New Hebrides, administered jointly by the UK and France?

28 Which sporting figure is the subject of the biographies *Nobody Ever Says Thank You* and *Provided You Don't Kiss Me*, and the novel *The Damned Utd*?

Three bonus questions on Queen Victoria

a. 'Such a cold, odd man'. Of which of her prime ministers did Queen Victoria say these words, though she is said to have mourned him 'as a father' when he died in 1852?

b. Prime Minister for almost ten years, to whom did Victoria and Albert give the disparaging nickname of 'Pilgerstein'?

c. 'The Queen bowed down with this misfortune.' These words describe Victoria's reaction to the death of which former Prime Minister, in 1881?

29 Which Dutch city gives its name to the treaties of 1713 that concluded British involvement in the War of the Spanish Succession?

Three bonus questions on volcanic rocks

a. From the Greek for 'fire' and 'broken', what term describes rocks made solely or primarily of volcanic material?

b. Ultimately from the Latin for 'smooth', what Italian word is used for rocks composed largely of pyroxene and plagioclase feldspar that are formed from molten magma cooled beneath the Earth's surface?

c. Volcanic tuff is a light porous rock chiefly consisting of the consolidation of what volcanic material?

30 'An attempt to create a privatised form of international censorship' was one verdict on a bill introduced into the US Congress in late 2011 and known as SOPA. For what do the letters SOPA stand?

Three bonus questions on 'secrets'

a. *The Secret Pilgrim*, John Le Carre's novel of 1990, sees the final appearance in print of which character, introduced in *Call of the Dead* in 1961?

b. The *Secret Notebooks* of which writer, who died in 1976, were published in 2009 and include two posthumously discovered stories, 'The Capture of Cerberus' and 'The Incident of the Dog's Ball', featuring perhaps her best-known character?

c. *The Secret Garden*, first published in serial form in 1910, is a novel for children by which Manchester-born author and playwright?

The Answers

1 Como
- **a.** Hue (HSI stands for hue, saturation and intensity)
- **b.** Candela
- **c.** White

2 The (Royal) Greenwich Observatory
- **a.** Great tit
- **b.** Dunnock / hedge sparrow / hedge accentor
- **c.** Chaffinch

3 North Korea
- **a.** Unemployment
- **b.** (Arthur M.) Okun (Okun's Law)
- **c.** Keynesian (unemployment)

4 Mu
- **a.** Good (it means 'Talk [is] Good')
- **b.** (Edward) Sapir and (Benjamin Lee) Whorf
- **c.** (Mandarin) Chinese

5 Kuiper Belt (Gerard Kuiper, 1905–1973)
- **a.** Pooh-Bah
- **b.** Short sharp shock ('Awaiting the sensation of a short sharp shock, / From a cheap and chippy chopper on a big black block')

> c. Lord Peter Mandelson (including Secretary of State for Business, First Secretary of State, Lord President of the Council, President of the Board of Trade, and Church Commissioner; he sat on thirty-five Cabinet committees and sub-committees)

6 Graham Greene
> a. Ironclad / iron-hulled
> b. Nuclear (reactor)
> c. Hydrofoil

7 Homeotic (genes)
> a. Senegal
> b. Cape Verde / Cap-Vert
> c. Mali

8 When x equals zero or y equals zero ($(x+y)2 = x2 + 2xy + y2$. Hence we have the equality $(x+y)2 = x2 + y2$ if and only if $2xy = 0$, i.e. if and only if $x = 0$ or $y = 0$)
> a. Twin Prime Conjecture (accept De Polignac's Conjecture, of which the Twin Prime Conjecture is a special case)
> b. Hilbert's Tenth Problem (accept Matiyasevich's Theorem or the M.R.D.P. Theorem, the latter denoting Matiyasevich, Robinson, Davis and Putnam. And the short answer is no, there isn't one.)
> c. Goldbach's Conjecture

9 Jar (Canopic jars used in ancient Egypt to hold the viscera of an embalmed body; Mason and Kilner jars used for preserves; Leyden jar was an early form of capacitor)
> a. Schiaparelli (Elsa and Giovanni respectively)
> b. Bellini (Vincenzo, Giovanni and Lorenzo)
> c. (Joseph) Grimaldi

10 James Joyce (*Ulysses*, after the character Leopold Bloom)
> a. *The Prime of Miss Jean Brodie* by Muriel Spark

   b.   1513 and Helsinki

   c.   'The Lady of Shalott'

11 Helium (He)

   a.   Fever (accept temperature / hyperthermia / pyrexia; some reduce fever by the means of reducing temperature)

   b.   (High) Blood pressure (hypertension)

   c.   Cholesterol

12 Cirque

   a.   Stendhal (Stendal in Saxony-Anhalt)

   b.   Colette (Sidonie Gabrielle Colette)

   c.   Molière

13 (Donato) Bramante (not Michelangelo, who took over St Peter's much later, in 1547)

   a.   (Lady) Godiva / Godgifu

   b.   (Gnaeus Julius) Agricola

   c.   Vulcan

14 Tonsure (Latin: *tondere*, 'shear')

   a.   Septuagint (*Interpretatio septuaginta virorum*, 'translation of the seventy interpreters')

   b.   Miles Coverdale ('Coverdale's Bible', c.1488–1569)

   c.   Balm / balme ('Is there no balm in Gilead?' 'Medicine' is used in some other versions)

15 Live Aid (NB not Band Aid, which was earlier)

   a.   (R.D.) Laing (Ronald David Laing)

   b.   *The Book of Dave*

   c.   (Bernhard) Schlink

16 Modulation

   a.   Axon

   b.   Anoxic

c.   Axis

17 John Brown (1800–1859)
   a.   Carlos Acosta
   b.   (Sir) Robert Helpmann
   c.   (Vaslav or Vaclav) Nijinsky

18 *Great Expectations, Bleak House, Hard Times, The Old Curiosity Shop, Our Mutual Friend* (*A Christmas Carol* is classed as a novella)
   a.   John F. Kennedy
   b.   Wynton Marsalis
   c.   Online / internet

19 Rodrigo Borgia / Alexander the Sixth (1431–1503)
   a.   St Anselm (of Canterbury)
   b.   William the Second
   c.   Doctor of the Church (the epithet 'Doctor Magnificus' is specific to him)

20 Bingo
   a.   *The Abduction from the Seraglio* (*Die Entführung aus dem Serail*; accept *The Escape from the Seraglio* as it is also known. Not the unfinished *Zaida*, which was not performed during Mozart's lifetime)
   b.   Louis de Bernières
   c.   Gallipoli

21 Borley (rectory)
   a.   Obelisk (not 'obelus', which cannot mean pillar)
   b.   (End of) Paragraph
   c.   Section (accept section sign / section mark; §, short for *signum sectionis*, section sign)

22 Middle East
   a.   Maya or Mayan
   b.   Guatemala

    c.   Venus (until its reappearance as a morning star in the same apparent position relative to the Sun as its previous reappearance)

23 *Antony and Cleopatra*
    a.   Mercury, bromine
    b.   Rubidium
    c.   Carbon (as diamond or graphite)

24 (Most Ancient and Noble) Order of the Thistle (accept but qualify Order of St Andrew)
    a.   Henley
    b.   Toxic
    c.   Grime

25 Internationals (in full International Working Men's Association)
    a.   Lorelei (she plays Lorelei Lee)
    b.   *The Seven Year Itch*
    c.   *Some Like It Hot* (she plays Sugar Kane)

26 Six
    a.   Hydrochloric acid (HCl)
    b.   Aqua fortis
    c.   Sulphuric acid (H_2SO_4)

27 Balti (Baltistan, Baltimore, Baltic)
    a.   New Caledonia
    b.   Papua New Guinea
    c.   Vanuatu

28 Brian Clough (1935–2004; biographies by Jonathan Wilson and Duncan Hamilton; novel by David Peace)
    a.   (Sir Robert) Peel
    b.   (Lord) Palmerston
    c.   (Benjamin) Disraeli

29 Utrecht
- **a.** Pyroclasts / pyroclastic
- **b.** Gabbro
- **c.** Ash

30 Stop Online Piracy Act
- **a.** (George) Smiley
- **b.** Agatha Christie
- **c.** Frances Hodgson Burnett

Match Seven

1 Which three letters, referring to a property of fractions, also denote a technology used in image projection or display?

Three bonus questions on mirrors for princes

a. The English poet and scholar John Skelton wrote a *Speculum Principis*, or treatise of advice and instruction, addressed to which future monarch to whom he was then tutor?

b. *The Education of a Christian Prince* is a treatise of 1516 dedicated to the future Holy Roman Emperor Charles the Fifth by which humanist and theologian?

c. *Basilikon doron*, meaning 'Royal Gift', was a treatise on government written for his son, the Duke of Rothsay, by which monarch?

2 At the same distance as Jupiter from the Sun and approximately 60 degrees ahead of it and 60 degrees behind it in their orbit, what name from Greek legend is collectively given to the asteroids Achilles, Nestor, Hektor and Patroclus?

Three bonus questions on the colour blue

a. In 1957, which artist registered the letters 'I. K. B.' as a trademark for the distinctive ultramarine colour he had used in nearly 200 of his blue monochrome paintings?

b. In which Moroccan city is the Majorelle garden, formerly owned by Yves St Laurent, and named after the French artist whose design for it used a distinctive shade of cobalt now named after him?

c. In 1999, the colour-matching company Pantone chose which shade of blue as its 'official colour of the millennium', describing it as 'the colour of the sky on a serene, crystal clear day'?

3 The impossibility of travelling around the Prussian city of Konigsberg on the River Pregel, crossing each of its seven bridges only once and returning to the point at which one started, was proved in 1736 by which Swiss-born mathematician?

Three bonus questions on the former East Germany

a. Subtitled *Stories from Behind the Berlin Wall*, which 2003 book by Anna Funder recounts the personal histories of some of those who lived under the threat of the GDR's state security?

b. Which historian wrote about the dossier the Stasi kept on him in his 1997 book *The File*? His other works include, in 2009, *Facts Are Subversive: Political Writing from a Decade Without a Name*?

c. A work of 2010 by Kai Schlüter reveals the efforts made by the Stasi to spy on which Nobel Prize-winning author, codenaming him 'Bolzen', as in 'bolt'?

4 In geology, what short term indicates the slow, imperceptible movement of soil and detritus downhill under the influence of gravity and processes such as successive freezing and thawing? It is also used for the continuous deformation of metal under stress, especially at high temperatures.

Three bonus questions on place-name elements

a. Meaning a spring or stream, what place-name element is found in the names of two south-coast seaside resorts, one in Dorset and the other close to Beachy Head?

b. Meaning a promontory, what four-letter element appears in the name of a Lincolnshire seaside resort, and the largest town on the Isle of Sheppey?

c. What Old English word meaning 'the church of a monastery' is found in the place names of an inner London borough and a Devon town noted for carpet-making?

5 Which savoury dish has a name derived from an Old French word for the blade of a sword or knife, or for a thin plate, possibly referring to its shape?

Three bonus questions on styles of French cooking

a. Meaning a garnish of lobster, truffles and Mornay sauce, 'à la Walewska' means in the style of a mistress of which military and political figure?

b. Which area in south-west France, now mostly in the Dordogne département, gives its name to a truffle-based sauce or truffle garnish?

c. Sharing its name with a French film director, which style means garnished with mushrooms and truffles?

6 In 2011, the former French government minister Christine Lagarde began a five-year term as Managing Director of which United Nations agency, whose aims include securing global financial stability and facilitating international trade?

Three bonus questions on words ending in '-verse'. In each case, give the word from the definition.

a. The side of a coin that bears a monarch's head or other symbol of state?

b. In anatomy, a plane that crosses the body at right angles to the coronal and sagittal planes?

c. The third word of the title of a 1982 work by Douglas Adams?

7 What two-word term was coined by the German-born psychologist of Danish extraction, Erik H. Erikson, to describe an inability to reconcile conflicting aspects of one's personality?

Three bonus questions on Trafalgar Square

a. His noted designs including the Houses of Parliament and Manchester Art Gallery, which architect remodelled Trafalgar Square from 1840?

b. In 1999, the first commission for the empty fourth plinth was *Ecce Homo*, a sculpture of Christ by which artist?

c. Which capital city has since 1947 donated a Christmas tree to Trafalgar Square, in recognition of Britain's support during the Second World War?

8 Awarded the Prix Goncourt in 2010, *The Map and the Territory* is a work by which controversial French author, whose previous works include *Platform* and *Atomised*?

Three bonus questions on a metal

a. Which soft metal, atomic number 78, has a high melting point, and is used for electrodes and for dishes in which materials can be heated to high temperatures, as well as in jewellery and dental alloys?

b. The Ostwald process, used in the production of fertilisers, is the oxidation of ammonia over a platinum catalyst to manufacture which acid?

c. The international prototype kilogram that is the standard unit of mass is made of platinum and which dense metal, with which it is often alloyed to increase its strength and hardness?

9 Answer as soon as you buzz. What is the minimal number of positive cubes needed to add together to make 23?

Three bonus questions on dental pathology

a. The Silness-Loe index, first published in 1964, is used in dentistry to measure levels of which substance?

b. Present in plaque, *mutans* and *sanguis* are species of a genus of which spherical gram-positive bacteria belonging to the phylum 'firmicutes'?

c. The calculus that forms when plaque hardens above or below the line of the gums is commonly known by which name?

10 A consequence of Noether's Theorem, the conservation of what physical quantity is associated with time invariance?

Three bonus questions on a French author

a. What was the pen-name of Amandine-Aurore Dupin, who is best known for her so-called 'rustic novels' including *The Devil's Pool* and *Little Fadette*?

b. Through her writing, George Sand brought to public attention the series of six allegorical tapestries given what title, dating to the Middle Ages and discovered by one of her lovers, the writer Prosper Merimee, in Boussac Castle in 1841?

> **c.** Sand's lovers also included which Polish-French composer and pianist? Their relationship lasted almost ten years and ended shortly before his death from tuberculosis in 1849.

11 Meanings of what five-letter word include: the membrane joining the cap to the stem of an immature mushroom; the margin of the bell of a jellyfish that helps in propulsion; and the retractable fabric awning used to shelter the audience in Roman theatres?

Three bonus questions on pairs of words that contain the same consonants in the same order, for example 'delta' and 'adult'. In each case, give both words from the definitions.

> **a.** 'Harsh, stern or severely simple' and 'gaze intently or obtrusively'?

> **b.** 'Device used to assist memory' and 'person pathologically obsessed with a single subject'?

> **c.** 'Halogen element, atomic number 53, used in solution as an antiseptic' and 'Norse deity known as "All-Father"'?

12 If potassium chloride is subjected to electrolysis, at which electrode will chlorine be liberated?

Three bonus questions on chemistry

> **a.** Which alkaline earth metal has an isotope, molecular mass ninety, produced as a by-product of nuclear fission?

> **b.** Strontium 90 presents a serious health hazard, since it may substitute for what element in bone?

> **c.** Strontium takes its name from the village of Strontian in western Scotland, where it was first discovered in ores of what metal?

13 'No praise is too high for him, in my view, and no celebration of his genius excessive.' These words of the Booker Prize winner Howard Jacobson refer to which novelist, on the bicentenary of his birth in early 2012?

Three bonus questions on novels that have won the Booker Prize. In each case, give the title of the work in which the following locations appear in the opening lines.

a. 'The Reading Room of the London Library' and 'Locked safe number 5'?

b. 'A fashionable apartment block ... on the edge of the ancient centre of Cracow'?

c. Darlington Hall?

14 In 1632, who painted the small portrait *Jacob de Gheyn the Third*? It is often called 'the world's most stolen painting', because of its theft from the Dulwich Picture Gallery on four occasions.

Three bonus questions on an artist

a. Known for an enthusiastic assessment of his own talent as 'close to Picasso', which US artist's works include many made by gluing plates to canvas and painting over them, such as the 1982 piece *Humanity Asleep*?

b. Schnabel made his directorial debut with a 1996 film about which Caribbean-American painter, who first came to notice as a graffiti artist, but died of a heroin overdose at the age of 27?

c. Which 2007 film by Schnabel was an adaptation of a memoir by the former Editor-in-Chief of *Elle* magazine Jean-Dominique Bauby, written after a stroke had paralysed all but his left eye?

15 Which tennis venue is named after the pioneering airman who became the first man to fly non-stop across the Mediterranean? He was killed when his plane was shot down in October 1918, the day before his 30th birthday.

Three bonus questions on hexagons

a. What natural product consists of a vertical lattice of rhombic decahedra with a hexagonal cross-section at the open end and walls less than 0.1 millimetre thick?

b. What name is given to the concept introduced by Linus Pauling in 1931 to explain why a benzene molecule is a regular hexagon, with six carbon-carbon bonds of equal length?

c. The earliest known paper to conjecture on the hexagonal structure of the snowflake, the 1611 essay entitled 'On the Six-Cornered Snowflake' was the work of which German astronomer?

16 Which US playwright describes the central image of his only novel, *Focus*, as being 'the turning lens of the mind of an anti-Semitic man forced by his circumstances to see anew his own relationships to the Jew'?

Three bonus questions on fountains

a. In which European city is the Jet d'Eau, which, with a jet of water rising to 140 metres, is one of the world's highest fountains?

b. Which fountain is believed to take its name from its location at the intersection of three roads, and is the largest of Rome's baroque water fountains?

c. In a fountain outside the Pompidou Centre in Paris, a nightingale, a mermaid and a firebird are among the sculptures representing the work of which Russian composer?

17 In aerodynamics, what adjective is generally used to describe speeds that are equal to or greater than Mach 5?

Three bonus questions on literary titles that contain numbers. In each case, complete the arithmetical calculations of the numbers in the titles of each pair of books. For example, Dickens' 'Cities' plus Dumas's 'Musketeers' gives the answer 'five'. Got it?

a. Gabriel García Márquez's 'Years of Solitude' multiplied by Tolkien's 'Towers'?

b. Hosseini's 'Splendid Suns' divided by T.S. Eliot's 'Quartets'?

c. Kurt Vonnegut's 'Slaughterhouse' multiplied by Arnold Bennett's 'Towns'?

18 A set of knotted cords hanging from a bar or central cord, the quipu was a counting device used by which ancient people of South America?

Three bonus questions on cruciferous plants

a. *Armoricia rusticana*, used in cooking, has a root which, when cut, produces an oil that irritates the eyes and sinuses, and has what common name?

b. *Lunaria* is cultivated for its flat translucent seed-pods, sometimes known as 'moon pennies', and has what common name?

c. *Isatis tinctoria*, a cruciferous plant that has been used to produce an indigo dye, has what common name?

19 '[This is] a film about our times. The Arab Spring, protest movements, the Tottenham riots – they're all there.' These words of Ralph Fiennes refer to a 2011 cinematic version of which play by Shakespeare, his directorial debut?

Three bonus questions on films of the 1950s

a. Born in Mississippi in 1897, which author's works include the 1940 novel *The Hamlet*, which was filmed in 1958 with Paul Newman, Joanne Woodward and Orson Welles under the title *The Long, Hot Summer*?

b. *Suddenly, Last Summer*, released in 1959 and starring Elizabeth Taylor and Katharine Hepburn, was based on the play of the same name by which US dramatist, born in 1914?

c. Later adapted as a stage musical entitled *A Little Night Music*, *Smiles of a Summer Night*, released in 1955, is by which Scandinavian director, born in 1918?

20 'In adolescence, I hated life and was continually on the verge of suicide, from which, however, I was restrained by the desire to know more mathematics.' These are the words of which future British Nobel laureate, in the 1930 work *The Conquest of Happiness*?

Three bonus questions on a classical work

a. Quote: 'Of shapes transformde to bodies straunge, I purpose to entreate, / Ye gods vouchsafe, (for you are they ywrought this wondrous feate) / To further this mine enterprise.' These lines are from Arthur Golding's 1567 translation of which classical work?

b. Premiered in 1718 as a one-act masque and later revised, which pastoral opera by Handel was based on a story in *Metamorphoses* and concerns the love of a nymph for a shepherd, the latter being murdered by the giant Polyphemus?

c. Which story in the *Metamorphoses* concerns two lovers who are forbidden to meet by their parents, and so communicate through a crack in the wall between their adjoining houses?

21 Cape Verde, Oman, St Lucia and Bangladesh are among countries that joined the United Nations during which decade?

Three bonus questions on error

a. First used by US astronauts to describe problems with electronic instruments, what slang term for a malfunction is thought to be derived from a Yiddish word for 'a slip'?

b. What word for a social blunder or faux pas is taken from a specialised use of a French word meaning an iron hook with a handle, used for landing large fish?

c. What term has come to be applied to a software error, and is commonly thought to have come from an incident involving a technician extracting a moth from a US Navy computer in 1947?

22 At the Battle of the Catalaunian Plains in AD 451, which king was defeated by a coalition of Visigoths under Theodoric and Romans under Flavius Aëtius?

Three bonus questions on historical events

a. Which historical event took place just after dawn on 28 April 1789 off the volcanic island of Tofua in the South Pacific?

b. In the years after the *Bounty* mutiny, William Bligh became captain of HMS *Director*, part of the fleet in which, in 1797, a mutiny occurred at which Royal Navy anchorage at the mouth of the Thames?

c. During the so-called 'Rum Rebellion' of 1808, discontented troops led by Lieutenant-Colonel George Johnston took Bligh into custody while he was serving as governor of which Australian state?

23 In a well-known portrait by the photographer Robert Howlett, which engineer is pictured in front of the giant chains of a braking mechanism used in the attempted launch of *The Great Eastern* from its dry dock at Millwall?

Three bonus questions on the names of railway stations

a. The full name of which English railway station refers to the meadows within the parish of a nearby church established by the Knights Templar in the twelfth century?

b. Which London railway terminus derives its name from a church built on the bank of a small stream, then called the Tyburn?

c. In which British city is the main railway station named after a series of novels published between 1814 and 1831?

24 What surname is shared by two men who were appointed Home Secretary within twelve years of each other, in 1992 and 2004 respectively?

Three questions on a politician

a. Defeated in the 1983 general election, which former Labour party leader died in 2010, aged 96?

    b.   Michael Foot's 1957 work *The Pen and the Sword* is a biography of which satirist, poet and cleric, born in Dublin in 1667?

    c.   During the 1960s, Foot published a two-volume biography of which politician, widely regarded as the father of the National Health Service?

25 'An eccentric and bohemian club, of which the absolute condition of membership lies in this, that the candidate must have invented the method by which he earns his living.' These words describe which fictional club, created by G.K. Chesterton in *The Tremendous Adventures of Major Brown*?

> **Three bonus questions on carelessness. I will read three extracts from well-known literary works. In each case, identify the author and the title of the work.**

    a.   'They were careless people, Tom and Daisy—they smashed up things and creatures and then retreated back into their money or their vast carelessness, or whatever it was that kept them together, and let other people clean up the mess they had made.'

    b.   'Who hath not seen thee oft amid thy store? / Sometimes whoever seeks abroad may find / Thee sitting careless on a granary floor, / Thy hair soft-lifted by the winnowing wind.'

    c.   'To lose one parent, Mr Worthing, may be regarded as a misfortune; to lose both looks like carelessness.'

26 Boston in 1897, New York in 1970, Berlin in 1974, Chicago in 1977 and London in 1981; what sporting event was initiated in these cities in these respective years?

Three bonus questions on host cities of the summer Olympic Games since the Second World War. In each case, identify the city from its geographical coordinates.

a. 41 degrees, 23 minutes north; 2 degrees, 11 minutes east?

b. 34 degrees, 3 minutes north; 118 degrees, 15 minutes west?

c. 33 degrees, 51 minutes south; 151 degrees, 12 minutes east?

27 Censured in 2004 for referring to the Queen as 'Mrs Windsor', Leanne Wood became, in March 2012, the first woman to lead which British political party?

Three bonus questions on the Welsh alphabet

a. The Welsh alphabet contains eight digraphs, or pairs of letters representing a single sound, which do not appear in the English alphabet; three consist of a double letter, with double-l being perhaps the most familiar. What are the other two?

b. In terms of dictionary entries, which digraph comes between 'c' and 'd' in the Welsh alphabet?

c. The Welsh alphabet regards seven letters as vowels: the 'a', 'e', 'i', 'o' and 'u' that also occur in the English alphabet, and which two additional letters?

28 In chemistry, what is the oxidation state of oxygen in hydrogen peroxide, that is, H_2O_2?

Three bonus questions on chemistry. I want to know the colour of the emission spectra, shown by a flame test, of the following S-block metals.

   a.   Calcium?

   b.   Barium?

   c.   Sodium?

29 Which group of widespread illnesses are caused by rhino-viruses, a genus of single-stranded RNA viruses containing around one hundred species?

Three bonus questions on conductors

   a.   Which German conductor began one of the most successful periods of his career when, in 1955, at the age of 70, he became music director of London's Philharmonia?

   b.   Which Dutch conductor was appointed music director of the Glyndebourne Festival in 1977, and in 1987 took up the same role at Covent Garden?

   c.   Sir Colin Davis is regarded as one of the foremost interpreters of which nineteenth-century French composer, having recorded works including *The Trojans* and *Harold in Italy*?

30 Although the observation of variation between populations of finches on the Galapagos Islands is better known, variation within birds of the family *Mimidae* was a key to Darwin's ideas on evolution. These birds have what common name?

Three bonus questions on primatologists

a. Which British primatologist's research in Tanzania includes the discovery that chimpanzees use tools in the form of sticks which they strip of leaves and use to take termites out of their mounds to eat?

b. Regarded as the foremost authority on orang-utans, which German-born scientist received the prestigious Kalpataru Award in 1977 from the Republic of Indonesia, given for outstanding environmental leadership?

c. Which American primatologist was, along with Goodall and Galdikas, a protégé of Louis Leakey and dubbed one of 'Leakey's Angels'? She was particularly associated with the study of the mountain gorillas of Rwanda.

The Answers

1 LCD (Lowest or Least Common Denominator; Liquid Crystal Display)

    a. Henry the Eighth (during the 1490s; the work is now lost)

    b. (Desiderius) Erasmus

    c. James the Sixth (of Scotland) (accept James the First, correcting it; it was written in 1599, four years before he inherited the English throne, and passed to the future Charles the First after the Duke of Rothsay's death)

2 Trojans

    a. Yves Klein (International Klein Blue)

    b. Marrakech (Jacques Majorelle, 1886–1962; Majorelle blue)

    c. Cerulean (blue)

3 (Leonard) Euler

    a. *Stasiland*

    b. (Timothy) Garton-Ash

    c. Günter Grass

4 Creep

    a. Bourne (Bournemouth and Eastbourne)

    b. Ness (Skegness and Sheerness)

    c. Minster (City of Westminster and Axminster; Old English: *mynster*)

5 Omelette (Old French: *amelette*)
- **a.** Napoleon (Bonaparte / the First)
- **b.** Perigord ('à la Perigourdine')
- **c.** À la Godard

6 International Monetary Fund / IMF
- **a.** Obverse (the 'tails' side is the 'reverse')
- **b.** Transverse (aka 'horizontal', 'axial' and transaxial', but these do not answer the question)
- **c.** Universe (*Life, the Universe and Everything*)

7 Identity crisis
- **a.** (Sir Charles) Barry
- **b.** Mark Wallinger
- **c.** Oslo

8 (Michel) Houellebecq
- **a.** Platinum
- **b.** Nitric acid (HNO_3)
- **c.** Iridium

9 Nine (8,8,1,1,1,1,1,1,1; working: 8 is the highest positive cube less than 23; we can add at most two 8s together before we exceed 23, so this is clearly the most efficient (minimal) representation.)
- **a.** Plaque
- **b.** *Streptococcus*
- **c.** Tartar

10 Energy
- **a.** George Sand
- **b.** *The Lady and the Unicorn*
- **c.** Frederic Chopin

11 Velum (Latin 'sail' or 'veil')
- **a.** Austere and stare
- **b.** Mnemonic and monomaniac

    c.   Iodine and Odin

⑫ Anode
    a.   Strontium
    b.   Calcium
    c.   Lead

⑬ (Charles) Dickens
    a.   *Possession (A Romance)* (A.S. Byatt, 1990 winner)
    b.   *Schindler's Ark* (accept 'Schindler's List', the title under which it was published in the USA and Commonwealth) (Thomas Keneally, winner in 1982)
    c.   *The Remains of the Day* (Kazuo Ishiguro, 1989 winner)

⑭ Rembrandt (van Rijn; the painting is nicknamed 'The Takeaway Rembrandt')
    a.   (Julian) Schnabel
    b.   (Jean Michel) Basquiat
    c.   *The Diving Bell and the Butterfly*

⑮ (Stade) Roland Garros
    a.   Honeycomb
    b.   Resonance (theory)
    c.   (Johannes) Kepler

⑯ Arthur Miller
    a.   Geneva
    b.   Trevi Fountain (Fontana di Trevi)
    c.   (Igor Fyodorovich) Stravinsky

⑰ Hypersonic (not transonic, which is Mach 0.8–1.2; not supersonic, which is anything above Mach 1; not high hypersonic, which is greater than Mach 10)
    a.   200 (100 x 2)
    b.   250 (1000 / 4)
    c.   25 (5 x 5)

18 Incas (accept Chimu, Caral, Caral-Supe, Wari)
   a. Horseradish
   b. Honesty
   c. Woad

19 *Coriolanus*
   a. William Faulkner (born Falkner)
   b. Tennessee Williams
   c. Ingmar Bergman

20 Bertrand Russell
   a. Ovid's *Metamorphoses*
   b. *Acis and Galatea*
   c. 'Pyramus and Thisbe'

21 1970s (1975, 1972, 1979, 1974)
   a. Glitch (first recorded use is by John Glenn in 1962)
   b. Gaffe
   c. Bug

22 Attila (the Hun)
   a. Mutiny aboard HMS *Bounty*
   b. The Nore (not the Spithead mutiny, which was in the same year, but Spithead is in the Solent)
   c. New South Wales

23 (Isambard Kingdom) Brunel
   a. Bristol Temple Meads
   b. Marylebone
   c. Edinburgh (Edinburgh Waverley, after the novels by Sir Walter Scott)

24 Clarke (Kenneth and Charles)
   a. Michael Foot
   b. (Jonathan) Swift
   c. (Aneurin) Bevan

25 The Club of Queer Trades
    a.   F. Scott Fitzgerald, *The Great Gatsby*
    b.   (John) Keats, 'Ode to Autumn'
    c.   (Oscar) Wilde, *The Importance of Being Earnest*

26 Marathon
    a.   Barcelona (in 1992)
    b.   Los Angeles (in 1984)
    c.   Sydney (in 2004)

27 Plaid Cymru
    a.   Double-d, double-f (dd, ff)
    b.   Ch
    c.   'W' and 'y'

28 Minus one (letter-h, 2, letter-o, 2)
    a.   Red (specifically brick red)
    b.   Green (specifically a pale yellow-green / apple green)
    c.   Yellow (or orange-yellow; accept orange)

29 (Common) Cold / respiratory tract infections
    a.   (Otto) Klemperer
    b.   (Bernard) Haitink
    c.   (Louis-Hector) Berlioz

30 Mockingbirds
    a.   (Dame) Jane Goodall
    b.   Biruté Galdikas
    c.   Dian Fossey

Match Eight

1 The name of which Asian island is spelt with the initial letters of the world's deepest lake, the world's highest waterfall, France's longest river and the UK's northernmost city?

Three bonus questions on nebulae named after animals

   a. Barnard 33 is a dark nebula within the larger nebula of Orion. What is its common name, after its resemblance to part of an animal?

   b. Another dark nebula, designated Barnard 72 in the constellation Ophiuchus, has what common name?

   c. A supernova explosion in the constellation of Taurus was observed on Earth in the year 1054; it left behind a pulsar rotating thirty times per second, and what surrounding nebula?

2 Published in 1591, five years after his death, *Astrophil and Stella* is a sonnet sequence by which poet?

Three bonus questions on seventeenth-century generals

   a. The son of a favourite of Elizabeth the First, who became the first Commander-in-Chief of the Parliamentary army in 1642, but resigned his commission in 1645?

b. Nicknamed 'Black Tom' in reference to his swarthy complexion, which Yorkshire-born soldier replaced Essex as commander, and led the Parliamentary army to victory at the Battle of Naseby in 1645?

c. Which general fought with Cromwell at the Battle of Dunbar in Scotland in 1650, but later played a key role in the restoration of Charles the Second?

3 Born in 1906, which playwright said of his best-known work that its early success 'was based on a fundamental misunderstanding. Critics and public alike insisted on interpreting in allegorical or symbolic terms a play which was striving all the time to avoid definition...'?

Three bonus questions on Christmas Eve

a. The treaty signed on Christmas Eve 1814, ending the 1812 war between the USA and Great Britain, is named after which town, now in Belgium?

b. Which North African country gained independence from Italy on Christmas Eve 1951, with King Idris the First as its monarch?

c. Christmas Island was discovered on Christmas Eve 1777 by which British navigator and explorer?

4 From the Greek meaning 'beside another plane surface', what term denotes a geometrical solid with six faces, each in the form of a parallelogram?

Three bonus questions on mathematics

a. What adjective is applied to a number which is not the root of any integer polynomial?

b. In 1882, the German mathematician Ferdinand von Lindemann proved the transcendence of Pi, and thereby obtained the first proof of the impossibility of which geometric construction, one of the three geometric problems of antiquity?

c. Nine years before Lindemann, the French mathematician Charles Hermite proved the transcendence of which ubiquitous mathematical constant?

5 Lamb, Love, Elliot, Bloch, Stokes, Rossby and Alfven are all types of what physical phenomenon?

Three bonus questions on a shared name

a. Which millenarian group of the 1650s believed that Christ's Second Coming was imminent, and took their name from their desire for a successor to the four empires of Assyria, Persia, Greece and Rome?

b. *Danaus plexippus*, commonly called the Monarch and noted for its lengthy migrations from Canada to Mexico, is a species of which insect?

c. Situated on the continental divide at an altitude of more than 11,000 feet, the Monarch Pass is in which US state?

6 Give the three words that begin the titles of all the following: a short story of 1911 by Willa Cather; a webcomic created by Nitrozac and Snaggy; a 1931 cookbook by Irma S. Rombauer; and a work by Dr Alex Comfort subtitled *A Gourmet Guide to Lovemaking*?

Three bonus questions on hotels and popular culture

a. Which field sport traces its origins to a meeting at the George Hotel in Huddersfield in 1895?

    b. First prepared in the original Raffles Hotel, which cocktail was invented by the barman Ngiam Tong Boon? Its ingredients include gin, cherry brandy, Benedictine and Cointreau.

    c. Agatha Christie was a regular guest at the Pera Palas Hotel in Istanbul, and is said to have written part of which 1934 novel in room 411?

7 Quote: 'You may not doubt that [this object], unwanted even in commercial America, is the deflowering of [our capital].' This statement concluded a protest by notable figures including Zola, Gounod and Dumas against the building of which structure in the late 1880s?

Three bonus questions on geology

    a. What term is derived from the German name for a region of Slovenia, and is given to a landscape lying over limestone which has been eroded by dissolution?

    b. Which North English dialect word denotes the clefts between the clints, or slabs, in limestone pavement?

    c. Grykes are produced when limestone is dissolved by which acid with the chemical formula H_2CO_3?

8 What primate links: a candidate put forward for election to Parliament in Thomas Love Peacock's novel *Melincourt*; the perpetrator of the crime in Edgar Allan Poe's 'The Murders in the Rue Morgue', and a librarian at the Unseen University in Terry Pratchett's *Discworld* series?

Three bonus questions on a French scientist

    a. The unit of optical frequency, equal to 10 to the 12 hertz, or 1 terahertz, is named after which French physicist?

b. Also named after Fresnel, what method is used in crystal optics to represent the doubly refracting properties of a crystal?

c. A Fresnel lens, used in lighthouses to concentrate the light into a relatively narrow beam, is characterised by a surface consisting of what?

9 Used from the 1920s onwards to describe art that incorporates movement or gives the illusion of movement, what term is used in physics for the energy of a body resulting from motion?

Three bonus questions on understanding, in the words of the King James Bible. In each case, identify the book of the Old Testament in which the following words appear.

a. 'And God gave Solomon wisdom and understanding exceeding much, and largeness of heart, even as the sand that is on the seashore.'

b. 'The race is not to the swift, nor the battle to the strong, neither yet bread to the wise, nor yet riches to men of understanding, nor yet favour to men of skill; but time and chance happeneth to them all.'

c. 'My mouth shall speak of wisdom; / And the meditation of my heart shall be of understanding.'

10 The Ariège, Tarn and Lot are among tributaries of which river? Rising in the Aran valley in the Pyrenees, it flows through Toulouse before joining the Dordogne to form the Gironde estuary.

Three bonus questions on rivers

a. The name of which river of Southern England begins words meaning 'principal male sex hormone' and 'evidence given in a court of law'?

b. The name of which Cornish river appears at the start of words meaning 'severe form of malaria' and 'Spanish fascist movement'?

c. The name of which West Country river begins words meaning 'critical interpretation of a text' and the stage direction for 'they go out'?

11 Thought to be the first of its kind in the world, a surcharge on foods that are high in saturated fat was introduced in October 2011 in which EU member state?

Three bonus questions on porridge

a. 'He receives comfort like cold porridge.' In which play by Shakespeare does Alonso's brother Sebastian say these words?

b. 'There's sand in the porridge and sand in the bed, / And if this is pleasure we'd rather be dead.' These words appear in 'The English Lido', a song from a 1928 revue by which dramatist, actor and songwriter?

c. 'We are not interested in the fact that the brain has the consistency of cold porridge.' These are the words of which pioneer of artificial intelligence, who died in 1954?

12 Meaning 'scattered', 'haphazard' or 'done at irregular intervals', which adjective shares its derivation with that of the group of Aegean islands which includes Skyros, Sciathos and Skopelos?

Three bonus questions on resignations

a. Commenting on the terms of a government recapitalisation plan effectively conditional on his resignation, which British banker observed in October 2008, 'This was more of a drive-by shooting than a negotiation'?

b. Lord Triesman resigned as chairman of England's bid to stage the 2018 World Cup after being recorded in secret in May 2010 suggesting that which two rival bidders might collude to bribe referees at the 2010 finals in South Africa?

c. After an enquiry in 2003 over financial mismanagement, who resigned as chief executive of Hollinger International, a global media empire that included the *Daily Telegraph*?

13 *The Death Ship* and *The Treasure of the Sierra Madre* are among the novels first published in German during the 1920s and 1930s under what penname, adopted by an author whose identity remains the subject of debate?

Three bonus questions on explorers

a. Which two British explorers became in February 1858 the first Europeans to reach Lake Tanganyika?

b. Meriweather Lewis and William Clark led the first US expedition across the American interior to the Pacific Northwest in 1804. What two-word term denotes the major territorial acquisition that they were to survey?

c. What were the surnames of the two explorers who led an expedition of 1860 to 1861 across Australia from the south to the far north? Both of them died on the return journey.

14 Which line of the London Underground has stations whose names may be described as the FA Cup winners in 1964, William Hague's constituency, an informal term for 'utterly mad', and the headquarters of the All England Lawn Tennis and Croquet Club?

Three bonus questions on early Anglo-Saxon kingdoms

a. Its name surviving in place names such as Wychwood and Wychavon, the kingdom of Hwicce was approximately coterminous with which English diocese?

b. Situated to the west and south of Hwicce, Magonsæte was absorbed into Mercia during the eighth century and was roughly coterminous with which diocese?

c. Its rulers described by one historian as 'the obscurest of English dynasties', the kingdom of Lindsey later gave its name to a subdivision of which county?

15 Of the kings of England between 1066 and 1603, the number of Henrys minus the number of Edwards gives the total number of kings with what regnal name?

Three bonus questions on words meaning 'very small'

a. Which synonym for 'very small' can also mean a letter in lower-case?

b. *Minium*, the Latin for 'cinnabar', was the origin of a verb meaning 'to paint with vermilion' or 'illuminate a manuscript', and thence, via an Italian art term, of which common word meaning 'very small'?

c. Which six-letter synonym for 'tiny' comes from the past participle of a Latin verb meaning to 'lessen'?

16 If the full name of 'W' begins with 't', with what letter does the full name of 'K' begin, in terms of chemical symbols?

Three bonus questions on mineralogy

a. What is the chemical name of the lead ore galena?

b. In the Goldschmidt classification of elements, what term is used of elements with an affinity for sulphur? Their ores are usually sulphides.

c. Its name derived from the Greek word *khalkos*, chalcocite is a sulphide ore of which metal, an important resource since prehistoric times?

17 'Blue Mauritius', 'Tyrian Plum', 'I.R. Official' and 'Inverted Jenny' are all rare examples of what collectors' items?

Three bonus questions on contemporary reviews of performances by the nineteenth-century actor Edmund Kean. In each case, identify the Shakespearean character he was portraying.

a. From 1814: 'Perhaps the accomplished hypocrite was never so finely, so adroitly portrayed; a gay, light-hearted monster, a careless, cordial comfortable villain.'

b. In a review of 1814, a critic complained that 'there was a lightness and vigour in his tread, a buoyancy and elasticity of spirit (unsuited to the character of) a man brooding over one idea, that of its wrongs, and bent on one unalterable purpose, that of revenge.'

c. From a review of 1815: 'He was cold, tame and unimpressive; Mr Kean was like a man waiting to receive a message from his mistress through her confidante, not like one who was pouring out his rapturous vows to the idol of his soul.'

18 Although actually fought on Breed's Hill, above Charlestown, Boston, what name is that usually given to the first pitched battle of the American War of Independence, in 1775?

Three bonus questions on coups d'état

a. In 2004, Mark Thatcher, the son of the former Prime Minister, was accused of backing a plot to overthrow the government of which small African country?

b. In 2006, which author admitted his involvement in a 1973 plot to overthrow the government of Equatorial Guinea in circumstances similar to the plot of his novel *The Dogs of War*?

c. A prima ballerina at Sadler's Wells and the Royal Ballet, which English dancer was revealed in 2010 to have been involved in a plot to overthrow the government of Panama in 1959?

19 The native language of the Nobel laureate Rabindranath Tagore and the cricketer Sourav Ganguly, what is the second most spoken language of India, and is often cited as the sixth most spoken worldwide?

Three bonus questions on public protest. In each case, name the Prime Minister who was in office when the following occurred.

a. 'Women's Sunday' on 21 June in Hyde Park, at which more than 200,000 gathered to demand women's suffrage?

b. The Jarrow March from Tyneside to London, protesting against unemployment?

c. The first Aldermaston march against nuclear weapons?

20 Appearing in the title of the heir to the Spanish throne, which autonomous community of Spain is known officially as a 'principality'? It is situated on the north coast between Cantabria and Galicia.

Three bonus questions on coastal regions

a. What name derives from that of the indigenous people of North Africa, and was used by Europeans until the nineteenth century for the coastal region of what is now Morocco, Algeria, Tunisia and Libya?

b. The Coromandel coast extends for more than 650 kilometres along the eastern seaboard of which country?

c. The British Gold Coast colony, which absorbed the Danish and Dutch Gold Coasts in the second half of the nineteenth century, became which independent West African nation in 1957?

21 Give all three of the rhyming words that mean: a narrow, propagating stream of particles or energy; the gaseous phase of water; and a concept that spreads via the internet?

Three bonus questions on fictional countries

a. Which oppressive republic is the setting for Margaret Atwood's novel *The Handmaid's Tale*, in which the only function of certain women is to breed children for infertile elite couples?

b. To which 'hitherto happy commonwealth' in Africa is the hero of Evelyn Waugh's novel *Scoop*, the journalist William Boot, sent to cover an expected revolution?

c. In C.S. Lewis's novel for children *The Horse and His Boy*, which country was established in the Narnian year 204 and is found far to the south of Narnia, below Archenland?

22 Which Indonesian city gives its name to a 1955 meeting of Asian and African countries that was a major step in the formation of the Non-Aligned Movement?

Three bonus questions on a Central Asian city

a. Thought to be one of the oldest continuously inhabited settlements in the world, which city on the historical Silk Road is the second-largest city of Uzbekistan?

b. Subtitled *A British Ambassador's Controversial Defiance of Tyranny in the War on Terror*, *Murder in Samarkand* is a 2006 work by which former diplomat?

c. Samarkand was the capital of which Turkic conqueror, born in 1336?

23 Which century links the appearance of Julian of Norwich's *Revelations of Divine Love*, Boccaccio's *Decameron*, Dante's *Divine Comedy* and Chaucer's *Canterbury Tales*?

Three bonus questions on mythological creatures

a. Derived ultimately from the Greek meaning 'snatcher', what name was given to the winged creatures who repeatedly stole the food of Phineas as part of his punishment by Zeus?

b. Quote: 'Their neck and count'nance, arm'd with talons keen / The feet, and the huge belly fledge with wings / these sit and wail on the drear mystic wood.' Which poet wrote this description of the harpies, in these lines in translation?

c. In Shakespeare's *The Tempest*, which character appears to Alonso, Sebastian and Antonio in the guise of a harpy and reproaches them for their treatment of Prospero?

24 The Andaman and Nicobar Islands, the Sunda Trench, and island nations, including the Comoros, Mauritius and the Maldives, all lie in which ocean?

Three bonus questions on bears

a. *Tremarctos ornatus*, the spectacled bear, has what alternative common name, after that of an extensive mountain range?

b. The name of which Asian peninsula appears in the binomial of the 'Sun bear' or 'Honey bear', native to lowland tropical rainforests?

c. Yosemite National Park in California is home to several hundred of which bear, whose scientific name is *Ursus Americanus*?

25 An abnormal craving for unusual foods common in pregnancy, and a font size now standardised as 12-point, are both denoted by what four-letter word, the Latin for 'magpie'?

Three bonus questions on the skin

a. Relating to their colour, what is the common two-word name of 'senile lentigo'? It is a benign condition caused after middle age by the long-term effects of sunlight upon exposed areas of the skin.

b. Often a normal vascular condition whose effects are exaggerated by exposure to the cold, 'livedo reticularis' is characterised by mottling seen on skin covering which part of the body?

c. What common term is usually applied to the cutaneous condition known in dermatology as 'striae gravidarum', and associated with pregnancy or rapid weight gain?

26 The hoist of the flag of Cameroon, the top strip of the flag of Iran, the bottom strip of the flag of Bolivia, and the fields of the flags of Bangladesh and Brazil are what colour?

Three bonus questions on apples

a. What term derives from the Latin for 'apple', and is given to the colourless crystalline acid involved in the Krebs cycle?

b. The English name for which soft fruit derives ultimately from the Latin for 'Persian apple', that is, *Persicum malum*?

c. *Malum granatum*, meaning 'many-grained apple', was the Latin name for which fruit, now known by an Anglo-Norman name with the same derivation?

27 What is the common name of the bird whose two families are the *Strigidae*, which include the Fearful, Elf and Spectacled species, and the *Tytonidae*, whose principal member in Britain is the Barn species?

Three bonus questions on right arms

a. The Japanese-American Daniel Inouye lost his right arm in Italy in the Second World War. He became President pro tem of the US Senate in 2010, after more than fifty years' continuous representation of which state?

b. What was the surname of the concert pianist for whom Maurice Ravel wrote 'Piano Concerto for the Left Hand'? The brother of a major philosopher, he lost an arm while serving with the Austrian army in the First World War.

c. In 1797, Horatio Nelson lost his right arm during an unsuccessful attempt to capture the port of Santa Cruz on which Atlantic island?

28 Which military unit was created by King Louis-Philippe in 1831 for the purpose of suppressing resistance to French rule in Algeria, with the provision that it should not be used on French soil?

Three bonus questions on the peace treaties of the First World War

- **a.** Ten weeks after the signing of the Treaty of Versailles with Germany in June 1919, which political entity formally ceased to exist as a result of the Treaty of Saint-Germain?

- **b.** The treaty with the new Republic of Hungary was not signed until June 1920, when the formal ceremony took place in which palace, built as a country retreat for Louis the Fourteenth in the park of Versailles?

- **c.** Which of the three allies known as the Entente Powers in 1914 did not sign the Treaty of Versailles with Germany in 1919?

29 In the subtitle of a 1947 book, what was defined by Stephen Potter as *The Art of Winning Games Without Actually Cheating*?

Three bonus questions on naughtiness. In each case, give the title and the author of the work in which the following lines appear.

- **a.** 'You are to live here for the next six months, learning how to speak beautifully, like a lady in a florist's shop ... If you're naughty and idle you will sleep in the back kitchen among the black beetles, and be walloped by Mrs Pearce with a broomstick.'

- **b.** 'In the afternoon the old lady was informed by every one that the shoes were red; and she said it was naughty and unsuitable, and that when Karen went to church in future, she should always go in black shoes, even if they were old.'

- **c.** 'Once at the number three, being the third number to be reached, then, lobbest thou thy Holy Hand Grenade of Antioch towards thy foe, who, being naughty in my sight, shall snuff it.' In which work of 1975 do these words appear?

30 After visiting Holland in the 1860s, the French art critic Théophile Thoré wrote a series of articles that championed which then-neglected Dutch painter as a poet of the everyday and a master of realism? His thirty-four authenticated works include *The Milkmaid*.

Three bonus questions on French cinema

a. Which French director made *Zéro de Conduite* and *L'Atalante* before dying in 1934 at the age of 29?

b. Shot in Nice and Paris during the Nazi occupation, which film by Marcel Carné is set in the world of nineteenth-century Parisian theatre and centres on the courtesan Garance and her lovers?

c. The son of a noted artist, who directed the 1939 film *La Règle du Jeu*, or *The Rules of the Game*?

The Answers

1 Bali (Baikal, Angel, Loire, Inverness)
- **a.** Horsehead (Nebula)
- **b.** Snake (Nebula)
- **c.** Crab (Nebula)

2 (Sir) Philip Sydney
- **a.** (Robert) Devereux / (Third Earl of) Essex
- **b.** (Sir Thomas) Fairfax
- **c.** (George) Monck / (First) Duke of Albemarle

3 Samuel Beckett (*Waiting for Godot*)
- **a.** Ghent (the Treaty of Ghent)
- **b.** Libya
- **c.** (Captain James) Cook

4 Parallelepiped (Greek: *parallelos*, 'beside another'; *epipedon*, 'plane surface'. Not 'rhomboid', which is usually 2-D and has a different derivation)
- **a.** Transcendental
- **b.** Squaring the circle (i.e. constructing a square equal in area to a circle using only straightedge and compass)
- **c.** E (accept 'the base of the natural logarithm' / 'Napier's constant')

5 Wave
- **a.** Fifth Monarchists / Fifth Monarchy Men
- **b.** Butterfly (or *Lepidoptera*)
- **c.** Colorado

6 'The Joy of...' ('The Joy of Nelly Deane', 'The Joy of Tech', *The Joy of Cooking*, *The Joy of Sex*)
    a. Rugby League (the formation of the Northern Rugby Football Union, renamed Rugby League in 1922, was announced there)
    b. Singapore Sling
    c. *Murder on the Orient Express*

7 The Eiffel Tower
    a. Karst
    b. Grykes / grikes
    c. Carbonic acid

8 Orang-utan
    a. (Augustin Jean) Fresnel
    b. Fresnel ellipsoid (accept 'ray ellipsoid', correcting it)
    c. Stepped concentric circles / rings / zones (or Fresnel zones)

9 Kinetic
    a. First Book of Kings (if they just answer 'Kings', press for the book as we've specified the King James Bible)
    b. Ecclesiastes (not 'Ecclesiasticus', of course)
    c. Psalms

10 Garonne
    a. Test (testosterone and testimony)
    b. Fal (falciparum and Falange)
    c. Exe (exegesis and exeunt)

11 Denmark (on foods that contain more than 2.3 per cent saturated fat, e.g. butter, cheese, pizza, meat, oil and processed food)
    a. *The Tempest* (II.i)
    b. Noël Coward
    c. (Alan) Turing

12 Sporadic
- **a.** Sir Fred Goodwin (of the Royal Bank of Scotland)
- **b.** Spain and Russia
- **c.** Conrad Black (Conrad Moffat Black, Lord Black of Crossharbour)

13 B. Traven (probably Otto Frege, aka Benick Traven Torsvan)
- **a.** (Sir Richard) Burton and (John) Speke (not Speke and Grant)
- **b.** Louisiana Purchase (and the territory beyond, as instructed by President Thomas Jefferson)
- **c.** (Robert O'Hara) Burke and (William John) Wills

14 District Line (West Ham, Richmond, Barking, Wimbledon)
- **a.** Worcester
- **b.** Hereford
- **c.** Lincolnshire

15 William (8 - 6 = 2; there were 3 Richards, 1 Stephen and 1 John)
- **a.** Minuscule
- **b.** Miniature
- **c.** Minute

16 P (W is tungsten, K is potassium)
- **a.** Lead sulphide (Lead(II) sulphide)
- **b.** Chalcophile (as opposed to lithophile [rock-loving], siderophile [iron-loving] or atmophile [gas-loving])
- **c.** Copper

17 Postage stamps
- **a.** Iago
- **b.** Shylock
- **c.** Romeo (referring specifically to his performance in the balcony scene)

18 (Battle of) Bunker Hill

a. Equatorial Guinea
b. Frederick Forsyth
c. Dame Margot Fonteyn (she was married to the Panamanian diplomat Roberto Arias, who attempted the coup)

19 Bengali
a. (H.H.) Asquith (1908)
b. (Stanley) Baldwin (1936)
c. (Harold) Macmillan (1958)

20 Asturias ('Prince of Asturias')
a. Barbary Coast (accept Barbary)
b. India (not New Zealand, which has the Coromandel Peninsular, which extends for only about 85 km)
c. Ghana

21 Beam, steam, meme
a. Gilead
b. Ishmaelia
c. Calormen

22 Bandung
a. Samarkand
b. Craig Murray
c. Tamerlane / Timur

23 The fourteenth century / 1300s (1373, 1344, 1308, 1387)
a. Harpies
b. Dante (Alighieri)
c. Ariel

24 Indian Ocean (the Nicobar Islands are in the Bay of Bengal, an arm of the Indian Ocean)
a. Andes (Andean bear)
b. Malay (*Ursus malayanus* / Malay bear)

    c.   (American) Black bear (not 'grizzly bear' [*Ursus arctos horribilis*] which is a brown bear; the park gets its name from a Native American word for 'grizzly bear' but it is no longer found there)

25 Pica

    a.   Liver spots
    b.   The legs / lower legs / feet
    c.   Stretch marks

26 Green

    a.   Malic acid
    b.   Peach
    c.   Pomegranate

27 Owl(s)

    a.   Hawaii
    b.   (Paul) Wittgenstein
    c.   Tenerife

28 (French) Foreign Legion / Legion Etrangère (original law that had excluded the Legion from French soil was suspended during Franco-German War in 1870)

    a.   Austria-Hungary (accept Dual Monarchy, Hapsburg Empire)
    b.   (Grand) Trianon (Treaty of Trianon)
    c.   Russia (Russia, France and the UK were the Entente Powers in 1914; the others joined later)

29 *Gamesmanship* (not *Lifemanship*, which was later, in 1950, or *One-Upmanship*, which was later still, in 1952)

    a.   *Pygmalion* by George Bernard Shaw
    b.   'The Red Shoes' by (Hans Christian) Andersen (in *Nye Eventyr / New Fairy Tales*, 1845)
    c.   *Monty Python and the Holy Grail*

30 (Johannes) Vermeer

a. (Jean) Vigo
b. *Les Enfants du Paradis / Children of Paradise*
c. (Jean) Renoir (his father was Pierre-Auguste)

Match Nine

1   Also noted for the Berners Street hoax and for sending the first picture postcard, the Victorian eccentric Theodore Hook launched which weekly publication in 1820, noted for its invective and high Toryism?

Three bonus questions on a place name

a.   The assizes of 1612 that tried most of the so-called Pendle Witches were held in which town of north-west England, granted city status in 1937?

b.   The Duke of Lancaster who was both the son of Edward the Third and the father of Henry the Fourth is usually known by what name, after his place of birth?

c.   Signed in 1979, the Lancaster House Agreement confirmed the independence of which African country from Great Britain?

2   Giving your answer as the actual value rather than an expression of it, what is the highest common factor of the following two numbers, given in their prime factorisation: two-to-the-power-one-hundred times three-cubed, and two-cubed times three-to-the-power-one-hundred?

Three bonus questions on schools of economic thought

a. The classical school of economic theory is generally held to have begun with the publication of which major work in 1776?

b. Emerging in the mid-nineteenth century, which school challenged the foundations of classical theory and saw capitalism as an evolutionary phase in economic development?

c. Flourishing in the USA during the 1920s, which school regarded individual economic behaviour as part of a larger social pattern influenced by contemporary ways of living and modes of thought?

3 In architecture, what term denotes ornamental plaster work applied to the façade of a rendered building? Particularly associated with East Anglia, it was revived in the nineteenth century by Norman Shaw and other arts and crafts architects.

Three bonus questions on wetland plants

a. Its cylindrical stalks used in weaving chair seats and in basketry, and its pith used as wicks in oil lamps, *Juncus* is a genus of over 200 species of plants commonly given what name?

b. *Phragmites australis* is the common species of which wetland plant, the dried stems of which have been used in thatching, in basketry, for arrows and pens, and in musical instruments?

c. Also known as reedmace or cat's tail, which plant of the genus *Typha* is used in northern India for ropes, mats, and baskets?

4 Formed from the union of the superior mesenteric and splenic veins, what three-word term denotes the specific vertebrate blood vessel which drains blood from the gastrointestinal tract to the liver?

Three bonus questions on biology

a. Found mainly in foods derived from animals, which of the B vitamins contains the element cobalt and is also known as cobalamin?

b. Which Group Two metal is found in the porphyrin ring of chlorophyll?

c. Which Group Eight metal readily converts between oxidation states, and is found in cytochromes of the electron transport chain?

5 Described as the 'Queen of the West' in a poem of 1854 by Longfellow, what is the third-largest city in Ohio, after Columbus and Cleveland?

Three bonus questions on the Chinese classics. I will read an extract from the opening lines of an English version of an ancient Chinese work. In each case, give the author to whom the text is generally ascribed.

a. 'The art of war is of vital importance to the state. It is a matter of life and death, a road either to safety or to ruin. Hence it is a subject of inquiry which can on no account be neglected.'

b. 'The way that can be spoken of is not the constant way; the name that can be named is not the constant name.'

c. '"To learn," said the master, "and then to practise opportunely what one has learnt – does not this bring with it a sense of satisfaction?"'

6 Answer as soon as you buzz. If a rope encircles the Earth at a height of one metre above the ground and is then pulled tight, how much slack will be left over?

Three bonus questions on adaptations of plays by Chekhov

a. *Winter Dreams*, a one-act ballet choreographed by Kenneth Macmillan, is based on which play by Chekhov?

b. *Wild Honey* by Michael Frayn is a reworking of which of Chekhov's plays? Discovered without a title page almost twenty years after Chekhov's death, it centres on a 'slightly married' provincial schoolmaster.

c. Tennessee Williams described his 1981 play *The Notebook of Trigorin* as a 'free adaption' of which play by Chekhov?

7 Born in the Spanish Basque country in 1770, the naval officer and ambassador Don Miguel Ricardo de Alava had the rare distinction of being present at which two crucial military events, both of which give their names to well-known locations in London?

Three bonus questions on oil companies

a. Shell, the global group of petrochemical companies formed by a merger in 1907, has its registered office in London but its headquarters in which European city?

b. The American Bob Dudley took over as BP's chief executive in autumn 2010 after the resignation of which Briton?

c. Having its headquarters in Dhahran, Saudi Aramco is one of the largest oil corporations in the world; for what does the acronym 'Aramco' stand?

8 Inspired by a character in Shakespeare's *Measure for Measure*, Tennyson wrote two poems whose titles contained which girl's name? One of these poems was later the inspiration for a painting by John Everett Millais.

Three bonus questions on US foreign policy

a. Which US President issued the 'doctrine' of 1823 that warned European nations against interference in the Americas?

b. The Truman doctrine of 1947 stated that the US would 'support free peoples who are resisting attempted subjugation by armed minorities or by outside pressures', and was directed initially at two Mediterranean countries. Name either.

c. The Carter doctrine of 1980 stated that the US would use military force if necessary to defend its interests in the Persian Gulf, and was a response to the Soviet invasion of which country?

9 *Erewhon*, the title of Samuel Butler's satirical novel of 1872, was chosen as a deliberate anagram of which word?

Three bonus questions on Victorian clergymen

a. William Buckland, who became Dean of Westminster in 1845, was a prominent contributor to which field of science?

b. Born in 1828, the Reverend Octavius Pickard-Cambridge was a noted authority on members of what terrestrial class of the phylum *Arthropoda*?

c. Built in the late 1870s by the Manchester clergyman George Garrett and designed for use in war, 'Resurgam' was a name given to two early vessels in what general category of watercraft?

10 What is the northernmost of the sea areas used in the UK in the Met Office's shipping forecasts?

Three bonus questions on plate tectonics

a. In plate tectonics, what term denotes the process by which one plate slides under another into the Earth's mantle?

b. Examples including those which struck the Kamchatka peninsula in 1737, 1923 and 1952, what name is given to extremely powerful earthquakes which occur characteristically at subduction zones?

c. Caused by the African plate subducting under the Eurasian plate, the megathrust earthquake of AD 365 had its epicentre on or near which Mediterranean island?

11 The Webster-Ashburton treaty of 1842 adjusted the boundary between New Brunswick in Canada and which US state?

Three bonus questions on literary quotations

a. Which of Shakespeare's characters says that he would as soon make his secret intentions known as he would, quote: 'wear my heart upon my sleeve / For daws to peck at: I am not what I am'?

b. In the 1862 poem 'A Birthday', who wrote 'My heart is like a singing bird / Whose nest is in a watered shoot / My heart is like an apple-tree / Whose boughs are bent with thick-set fruit'?

c. In the 1855 poem 'De Gustibus', Robert Browning claimed, 'Open my heart and you will see / Graved inside of it ...' the name of which country, where he and Elizabeth Barrett Browning lived from 1846?

12 The Italian word *pigrizia*, the German *faulheit* and the French *paresse* indicate which negative human attribute, closely associated with one of the Seven Deadly Sins?

Three bonus questions on a religious movement

a. From a Dutch word meaning 'mumbler', what term was used from the fourteenth century for those radical Christians who held opinions similar to the reformer John Wyclif?

b. A reaction to the Lollards, Henry the Fourth's statute 'De Heretico Comburendo' legitimised what penalty for heresy, to be carried out by the secular authority?

c. Sir John Oldcastle, who led a Lollard rebellion in 1414, is often said to be the model for which character in Shakespeare's *Henry the Fourth Part One* and *Part Two*, and *Henry the Fifth*?

13 'King Stephen', 'The Ruins of Athens', 'Coriolan' and 'Egmont' are among the overtures of which composer, born in Bonn in 1770?

Three bonus questions on a medical condition

a. What Greek-derived term describes an abnormal state, resembling a trance, in which a person is apparently or actually unconscious and the muscles become rigid?

b. Which Greek philosopher is thought to have suffered from catalepsy because of his habit of standing fixedly when consulting his 'inner voice', or *daimonion*?

c. In which novel by Charles Dickens does Mrs Snagsby become cataleptic and need 'to be carried up the narrow staircase like a grand piano'?

14 Listen carefully. Words meaning 'hold close as a way of showing affection', 'stick used as a weapon' and 'partly-digested food in the mouth of a ruminant' are among the small number of dictionary headwords that begin with which three letters?

Three bonus questions on Indian states

a. Panaji is the capital of which small state on the Arabian sea? It was ruled by Portugal until 1961.

b. Chandigarh in north-west India is a union territory that is also the capital of two states; one is Haryana; what is the other?

c. Dispur is the capital of which state? Bounded to the north by the kingdom of Bhutan, it produces about half of the country's tea?

15 Give not the nationality but the name of the national anthem of which the first words, in translation, are: 'Arise children of the fatherland, the day of glory has arrived. Against us tyranny's bloody standard is raised.'

Three bonus questions on an item of apparel

a. Deriving from a Greek term appearing in the Gospel of Mark, sindonology is the term denoting the study of what specific item?

b. In the *Odyssey*, for whom was Penelope weaving a shroud while she waited for the return of Odysseus?

c. Of which country has it been remarked that there were parts of it where the only concession to gaiety was a striped shroud?

16 The birthplace of Karl Marx in 1818, which German city close to the border with Luxembourg is the location of the Porta Nigra gate and a basilica that is the largest intact Roman structure outside Rome?

Three bonus questions on autobiographical works by Russian authors

a. Published in the 1850s, the novels *Childhood*, *Boyhood* and *Youth*, about the son of a wealthy landowner, are early semi-autobiographical works by which Russian author?

b. *The House of the Dead*, published in 1862 and concerning life in a Siberian labour camp, is by which author, based in part on his own experiences of imprisonment for membership of the Petrashevsky circle of those opposed to Tsarism and serfdom?

c. In the memoir *The Oak and the Calf*, which Russian author describes his attempts to get his novels, including *Cancer Ward* and *The First Circle*, published in his own country?

17 Listen carefully and answer as soon as your name is called. The distinctive tricolour flag of the liberation leader Francisco de Miranda forms the basis of the national flags of three Latin American countries. For ten points, name two of them.

Three bonus questions on national flags

a. Similar to that of Texas, which country's flag consists of two unequal horizontal bands of white and red; in the canton is a blue square with a white, five-pointed star?

b. The national flag of which Caribbean country consists of blue and white horizontal stripes with a red triangle at the hoist on which there is a white, five-pointed star?

c. Resembling that of the USA, the flag of which African country consists of horizontal red and white stripes with a single white star in a blue canton?

18 Terms meaning a very small amount of money, an alarmist person, a light wire mesh and a cowardly disposition are linked by which bird?

Three bonus questions on the classification of birds

a. To which order of birds do owls belong?

b. Which bird, having only one species, belongs to the order *Struthioniformes*?

c. Within the order *Columbiforme*, the family *Columbidae* comprises birds known generally by two common names. Give either of them.

19 In marine biology, what term indicates inhabitants of the sea beyond the edge of the continental shelf, specifically where it is deeper than 200 metres?

Three bonus questions on Irish food festivals

a. Since 1954, Galway has held an annual festival celebrating the opening of the season for which marine bivalve molluscs?

b. Sometimes called the gourmet food capital of Ireland, which fishing port on the west coast of Cork holds a food festival every October?

c. Held at the Bistro Martello on 16 June, the offal-based 'Bloomsday Breakfast' is one of many Dublin events celebrating which novel?

20 'Grey beard' for an older person and 'wheels' for a car are examples of which figure of speech, whose Greek-derived name means 'taking up together'?

Three bonus questions on torments in the Underworld, according to Homer's *Odyssey*

a. Punished for assaulting Leto, Tityus is seen by Odysseus as an enormous figure covering nine acres of land in Hades, and being subjected to what particular torment?

b. His name used adjectivally to mean 'endlessly laborious', which evildoer was, according to Homer, condemned to roll an immense boulder uphill only to watch it roll down again, and to repeat the task perpetually?

c. Which Lydian king killed his son Pelops and offered his flesh to the gods? In the Underworld, fruit and water eternally receded from him when he tried to reach for them.

21 Listen carefully. What is the limit of the sequence n to the power ten all divided by ten to the power n, as n tends to infinity?

Three bonus questions on scientific terms

a. Dermatoglyphics, used as a means of identification and as a genetic indicator, is the scientific study of what?

b. Comprising two extant species and resident in Southeast Asia, *Dermoptera* is an order of arboreal gliding mammals known by what common name?

c. Dermatophytosis is a clinical condition caused by a fungal infection of the skin in humans and some animals, and is commonly known by what name?

22 Consisting of a structural core of fibroin surrounded by a matrix of serecin, what protein fibre is produced by the larva of the insect that has the binomial *Bombyx mori*?

Three bonus questions on dietetics

a. Marasmus and kwashiorkor are childhood diseases caused by deficiency of which major nutrient?

b. What name is thought to derive from the Sinhala meaning 'I can't, I can't', and is caused by deficiency of thiamine?

c. Endemic goitre is caused by dietary deficiency of which element?

23 The Yorkshire-born physician John Snow is often regarded as the father of modern epidemiology for his investigations into the 'Broad Street pump' outbreak of which disease in London in 1854?

Three bonus questions on a scientist

a. Which scientist gives her name to the prominent medical, biological and biophysical research institute in Paris that she founded, along with Claudius Regaud, in 1921?

b. 'We believe the substance we have extracted from pitch-blende contains a metal not yet observed.' What did Marie Curie call this new element, after the place of her birth?

c. In 1903, Marie and Pierre Curie shared the Nobel Prize for Physics with which French scientist, who gives his name to the SI derived unit of radioactivity?

24 Listen carefully. The course record for the University Boat Race is 16 minutes 19 seconds, set by Cambridge in 1998. To the nearest whole Astronomical Unit, how far does sunlight travel in this time?

Three bonus questions on physics

a. What is the linear speed of a particle rotating in a circle with radius r and angular velocity omega?

b. What is the radial component of its acceleration?

c. If the particle has mass m, what is its moment of inertia about the axis of rotation?

25 The period of constitutional monarchy in France from 1830 to 1848 is often known by what two-word term, after the month in which the Bourbon King Charles the Tenth was overthrown?

Three bonus questions on political figures born in 1911

a. Born in the Auvergne in 1911, who succeeded Charles de Gaulle as President of France in 1969?

b. 'He served the Soviet Union more ardently than the Soviet leaders themselves did.' These words describe Todor Zhivkov, ruler of which country from the 1950s to 1989?

c. 'A triumph of the embalmer's art' was Gore Vidal's description of which US President, born in 1911?

26 In aeronautics, for what do the letters S-T-O-L stand?

Three bonus questions on quotations. For each answer, I want you to give me the title of a novel and its author. The title will be the words that complete each of the following lines.

a. 'I will show you something different from either / Your shadow at morning striding behind you / Or your shadow at evening rising to meet you; / I will show you fear in ...'?

b. 'Away! Away! For I will fly to thee, / Not charioted by Bacchus and his Pards, / But on the viewless wings of poesy, / Though the dull brain perplexes and retards: / Already with thee! ...'?

  c. 'Any man's death diminishes me, because I am involved in mankind, and therefore, never send to know ...'?

27 In astronomy, the abbreviation SMC stands for which satellite galaxy of the Milky Way, about 60,000 parsecs distant?

Three bonus questions on space exploration

  a. What object is less than 1,000 kilometres in diameter, accounts for almost a third of the mass of the Asteroid Belt, and in 2006 was classified as a dwarf planet?

  b. What name was chosen for the NASA spacecraft which entered the orbit of Ceres in March 2015, reflecting the mission's aim of providing information about the origins of the Solar System?

  c. The Dawn mission is a 'first' in space exploration because it examined two celestial bodies in succession, of which Ceres was the second; which asteroid was the first?

28 Renowned for its exact facial proportions, one of the best-known exhibits of the Neues Museum in Berlin is a limestone and plaster bust of which Egyptian queen of the 18th Dynasty, the wife of the Pharaoh Akhenaton?

Three bonus questions on sociology

  a. In an eponymous work of 2000, the Polish sociologist Zygmunt Bauman coined what two-word term to describe a contemporary society of seductive consumerism, rapid technological change, contingency and ambiguity?

b. Now used of reorganisation in business, what term did the German sociologist Max Weber use to describe the process in which modernisation affects economic life, law and religion by eliminating traditional ideas and customary practices?

c. In his 1900 work *The Philosophy of Money*, which German sociologist explored the connection between modernity and the development of a money economy?

29 Which EU member state shares its name with the palace that was used for the Paris peace conference of 1946 and later became the seat of the French senate?

Three bonus questions on the IUPAC systematic names of organic compounds derived from ethane, C_2H_6

a. What is the systematic name of the compound theoretically derived from ethane by replacing one hydrogen atom with an 'OH' group?

b. What is the systematic name of the compound derived from ethanal by replacing the final hydrogen atom on the substituted carbon with an 'OH' group?

c. What is the systematic name of the compound derived from ethanal by replacing the final hydrogen atom on the substituted carbon with an 'NH_2' group?

30 In philosophy, what Latin phrase is used for knowledge that can be derived from pure reasoning without reference to experience?

Three bonus questions on pairs of words that are easily confused. In each case, give both words from the definition. All three words end in the letters '-ious'.

    a. 'Superficially plausible but wrong in reality' and 'sham, bogus, fake or inauthentic'?

    b. 'Lewd or liable to arouse lust' and 'health-giving, wholesome or agreeable'?

    c. 'Progressing inconspicuously but harmfully' and, of an action or task, 'likely to incur or excite ill will or resentment'?

The Answers

1 *John Bull* magazine
- **a.** Lancaster (most were tried there, others in York)
- **b.** John of Gaunt
- **c.** Rhodesia, Zimbabwe

2 216 (basically, it's 2 to the 3, times 3 to the 3)
- **a.** (*The*) *Wealth of Nations* (by Adam Smith)
- **b.** Marxist (school)
- **c.** Institutionalist (school / economics)

3 Pargeting
- **a.** Rush / rushes (not bulrush)
- **b.** Reed (accept water reed)
- **c.** Bulrush

4 Hepatic portal vein / vena portae hepatic
- **a.** Vitamin B12
- **b.** Magnesium
- **c.** Iron

5 Cincinnati (the poem is 'Catawba Wine')
- **a.** Sun-tzu / Sunzi (*The Art of War*)
- **b.** Lao-tzu / Laozi (*Dao de Jing*)
- **c.** Confucius (*Analects*)

6 2 pi metres (allow 6.284 m)
- **a.** *The Three Sisters*
- **b.** *Platonov*

      c.   *The Seagull*

7 (Battles of) Trafalgar and Waterloo (fighting against the British on the former occasion, and with them on the latter)
- **a.** The Hague (reflecting the major shareholding of Royal Dutch Shell at the time of the merger)
- **b.** Tony Hayward
- **c.** Arabian American Oil Company

8 Mariana ('Mariana' and 'Mariana in the South'; Millais's painting was entitled *Mariana*)
- **a.** (James) Monroe
- **b.** Greece and Turkey
- **c.** Afghanistan

9 'Nowhere'
- **a.** Geology / palaeontology (accept either)
- **b.** Arachnids (specifically spiders, so accept this)
- **c.** Submarines

10 Southeast Iceland
- **a.** Subduction
- **b.** Megathrust (earthquake)
- **c.** Crete

11 Maine
- **a.** Iago
- **b.** Christina Rossetti
- **c.** Italy

12 Laziness / indolence / sloth
- **a.** Lollards (Dutch: *lollen*)
- **b.** Burning (at the stake)
- **c.** (Sir John) Falstaff

13 (Ludwig van) Beethoven

    a. Catalepsy
    b. Socrates
    c. *Bleak House*

14 Cud (cuddle, cudgel, cud)
    a. Goa
    b. Punjab
    c. Assam

15 'La Marseillaise'
    a. Shroud of Turin
    b. Laertes (accept Odysseus' father / her father-in-law)
    c. Wales (the dramatist Gwyn Thomas)

16 Trier / Treves
    a. Leo Tolstoy
    b. Fyodor Dostoevsky
    c. Aleksandr Solzhenitsyn

17 Colombia, Ecuador, Venezuela (the colours are blue, yellow and red)
    a. Chile
    b. Cuba
    c. Liberia

18 Chicken (chicken feed, Chicken Little, chicken wire, chicken-hearted or just chicken)
    a. *Strigiformes*
    b. Ostrich
    c. Pigeon and dove (the two are used somewhat interchangeably; ornithologically, dove tends to be used for smaller species)

19 Oceanic ('neritic' refers to marine life over the continental shelf, or where the sea is shallower than 200 metres)
    a. Oysters (Galway International Oyster Festival)
    b. Kinsale

    c.   *Ulysses*

20 Synecdoche (part used for whole, or vice versa)
- **a.** Vultures tear at his liver
- **b.** Sisyphus
- **c.** Tantalus

21 Zero ($n10/10n$)
- **a.** Fingerprints (accept skin markings; not 'skin')
- **b.** Colugos / cobegos (accept flying lemurs)
- **c.** Ringworm (accept tinea)

22 Silk
- **a.** Protein
- **b.** Beri-beri (also known as Wernicke-Korsakoff Syndrome but that doesn't answer the question)
- **c.** Iodine

23 Cholera
- **a.** Marie Curie
- **b.** Polonium
- **c.** (Antoine Henri) Becquerel

24 Two AU (nearly 186 million miles; sunlight takes 8 minutes 19 seconds to travel from the Sun to the Earth)
- **a.** R times omega / r omega / omega r
- **b.** R times omega squared / r omega squared / omega squared r
- **c.** M times r squared / m r squared

25 July Monarchy
- **a.** (Georges) Pompidou
- **b.** Bulgaria
- **c.** (Ronald) Reagan

26 Short Take-Off and Landing

a. *A Handful of Dust* by Evelyn Waugh (from Part One of T.S. Eliot's *The Waste Land*)

b. *Tender Is the Night* by F. Scott Fitzgerald (from Keats's 'Ode to a Nightingale')

c. *For Whom the Bell Tolls* by Ernest Hemingway (from John Donne's 'Meditation 17')

27 Small Magellanic Cloud

a. Ceres (not Eris, which lies in the Kuiper Belt and is larger)

b. Dawn

c. Vesta

28 Nefertiti

a. Liquid modernity

b. Rationalisation

c. (Georg) Simmel

29 (Grand Duchy of) Luxembourg (Palais du Luxembourg / Luxembourg palace)

a. Ethanol

b. Ethanoic acid (if they say acetic acid, ask for the systematic name)

c. Ethanamide (if they say acetamide, ask for the systematic name)

30 A priori ('a posteriori' refers to knowledge gained from experience)

a. Specious and spurious

b. Salacious and salubrious

c. Insidious and invidious

Match Ten

1 Taking its name from a county in Kentucky, which variety of alcoholic spirit shares its name with a family that ruled France, Naples and Spain?

Three bonus questions on the French Revolution. In each case, give the year in which the following took place.

   a. An armed Parisian mob stormed the Bastille on 14 July?

   b. Louis the Sixteenth and Marie Antoinette were both executed?

   c. The 'Reign of Terror' ended with the fall of Robespierre?

2 *The Rise and Fall of Music Hall* and *More Than a Game: The Story of Cricket's Early Years* are works by which political figure, who left the House of Commons at the 2001 general election?

Three bonus questions on volcanoes

   a. From the Greek for 'ash', what term denotes any dust or rock fragments which have been ejected into the air by a volcanic eruption?

   b. What term is used to describe the light porous rock formed by consolidated volcanic ash?

c. Deriving in part from Greek terms meaning 'fire' and 'broken in pieces', what term denotes hot, very fast-moving tephra that rolls down the sides of a volcano and along the ground during an eruption?

3 In the King James Bible, what is the third book of the Pentateuch?

Three bonus questions on ships

a. The *Olympic* and the *Britannic* were sister ships of which ocean liner, launched in May 1911?

b. The *Mayflower* was scheduled to sail from England in 1620 with which other ship, found en route to be unseaworthy? It shared its somewhat inappropriate name with a small blue flower.

c. Which ship was named after a Roman province of north-western Africa, and was the sister ship of the *Lusitania*, sunk by a U-boat in 1915?

4 *Chushingura* is one of the most familiar stories of which country? The term refers to fictionalised accounts of forty-seven warriors who avenge the death of their lord, who has been forced by a corrupt official to take his own life.

Three bonus questions on the size of Scotland

a. The UK has an area of around 244,000 square kilometres. What is the area of Scotland? You can have 5,000 square kilometres either way.

b. Which US state, one of the original thirteen colonies, has an area closest to that of Scotland?

c. Of the 27 member states of the EU, which landlocked state has an area closest to that of Scotland?

5 What short word links a central American republic; a city of west Texas on the Rio Grande, and a fabled city of gold sought by Spanish conquistadors?

Three bonus questions on geography

a. The Strait of Sicily, or Sicilian Channel, lies between Italy and which country?

b. The Soya Strait, or La Perouse, separates the Russian island of Sakhalin from which island of similar size?

c. The Strait of Hormuz separates Iran from the Musandam Peninsula, an exclave of which country?

6 Which major city shares its name with that of the most populous county in the United States of America, with nearly ten million inhabitants?

Three bonus questions on Irish literature

a. 'The cattle raid of Cooley' and 'Bricriu's Feast' are found in which cycle of stories, sometimes called the *Ulaid*, about the heroic age of the people of north-eastern Ireland?

b. Born in 1865, which Irish poet wrote the verse plays *Deirdre* and *The Death of Cuchulain*, both drawn from the Ulster Cycle?

c. The Fenian Cycle of stories, found in the *Book of Leinster* and the *Book of the Dun Cow*, centres on which hero and his war band, the Fianna Éireann?

7 Originally published in 1979 by Software Arts, a company founded by Dan Bricklin and Bob Frankston, VisiCalc was the first commercial program of what type to be made available to users?

Three bonus questions on spices in Asian cuisine

a. What common name is given to the eight-pointed fruit of the Chinese tree *Illicium verum*? When dried, it forms an ingredient of 'five-spice' powder.

b. An ingredient of Thai curry pastes, which member of the ginger family is used for its roots and comes in greater, lesser and *Kaempferia* varieties?

c. What is the common name of *Curcuma longa*, a member of the ginger family formerly known as Indian saffron?

8 What two-word name describes the specific fallacy found in the invalid syllogism: 'All students are idle; Henry is idle, therefore Henry is a student'?

Three bonus questions on philosophy

a. Calling it 'cupiditas', what was described by Spinoza as 'nothing else than the very essence or nature of man'?

b. Its title originally meaning 'drinking party', in which work by Plato is Socrates able to lead Agathon to concede that love or desire exists only in relation to some object that it lacks?

c. Which seventeenth-century French philosopher described desire as 'an agitation of the soul' that disposes itself to possess things it sees as agreeable but does not possess?

9 Pronounced differently in each case, which sequence of five letters ends three common words meaning 'vocalist', 'digit' and 'red-haired'?

Three bonus question on the circles of Hell in Dante's 'Inferno'

a. In the second circle of Hell, Dante finds Cleopatra, Helen of Troy and Queen Dido; what is their specific sin?

b. 'Cruel monster, fierce and strange, / Through his wide threefold throat barks as a dog / Over the multitude immers'd beneath'; in these lines Dante is describing which creature watching over those guilty of gluttony, although in classical mythology he guards the gates to Hades?

c. Located within the fifth circle of Hell, what is the name of the city of the dead, whose walls are protected by fallen angels?

10 Which association of states, established in 1949, currently has 47 members, and seeks to develop common and democratic principles throughout Europe based primarily on the European Convention on Human Rights?

Three bonus questions on expressions in which the last two letters of the first word and the first two letters of the second word are the same, for example 'apple lemonade' or 'tomato torte'. In each case, give the name of the food or drink from the definition.

a. Italian-style ice cream flavoured with *Citrus sinensis*?

b. Young soy beans served in their pods and prepared above boiling water?

c. A quickly cooked dish made from beaten eggs and edible fungi?

11 What six-letter adjective links titles of works by Sebastian Barry, Donna Tartt and Frances Hodgson Burnett?

Three bonus questions on boots in literature. Identify the author of the following lines in each case.

a. 'O Jonny, the power of your boot / And the accurate heart-stopping route / Of your goal as it ghosts / Through Australian posts / Is a triumph we gladly salute.'

b. 'Every woman adores a fascist, / The boot in the face, / The brute brute heart of a brute like you.'

c. 'If you want a picture of the future, imagine a boot stamping on a human face – for ever.'

12 From a Latin ablative singular form, which preposition links the last three letters of the English names of a landlocked South American republic and the country between Lithuania and Estonia?

Three bonus questions on a country

a. 2009 saw the death of Omar Bongo, Africa's longest-serving leader, who had been president of which oil-rich nation for over four decades?

b. Gabon is one of the world's foremost producers and exporters of which hard, brittle transition metal, extracted mainly from the ore pyrolusite?

c. On which inlet of the eastern Atlantic does Gabon lie?

13 What was the surname of the two Chancellors of the Exchequer, father and son, who died on the same date exactly seventy years apart? The father died in 1895, while the son later became Prime Minister.

Three bonus questions on marine invertebrates

a. What is the two-word common name of *Holothuroidea*, a class of echinoderms that are prized in South Asian cuisine, and known in Indonesia as *trepang*?

b. What is the two-word common name of *Pleurobrachia*, a genus of oval-shaped comb jellies covered with rows of small cilia?

c. Often brightly coloured with long tentacles, what is the common name of the order *Actiniaria*?

14 A powerful reducing agent used as a rocket fuel and in preparing polymer foams, which toxic flammable liquid has the chemical formula N_2H_4?

Three bonus questions on flame tests

a. Selenium, lead and arsenic all burn with flames of what colour?

b. Which element constitutes eight per cent of the Moon's crust, is the fifth most abundant element in the Earth's crust, and burns with a flame usually described as brick red?

c. Which soft, silver-white, highly reactive element was the first to be isolated by electrolysis, and burns with a lilac flame?

15 Meanings of what precise noun include: in phonetics, the exhalation of breath when articulating a sound and, in more general speech, a hope or ambition of achieving something?

Three bonus questions on eye rhymes, that is, pairs of words that end in the same letters but do not rhyme, for example 'champagne' and 'lasagne'. In each case, give both words from the definitions.

a. 'Organ between the oesophagus and small intestine' and 'leafy vegetable associated with Catherine de' Medici'?

   b.   'Biochemical compound such as actin, keratin or
            collagen' and 'title character of a novel by Mary
            Shelley'?

   c.   'Stanza or poem of four lines' and 'rank between
            Commander and Commodore'?

16 Yuka Sato of Japan won the first gold medal at which
major sporting and cultural event, inaugurated in
Singapore in August 2010? The next one was held in
Nanjing in 2014.

Three bonus questions on unusual world championships

   a.   A wrestling championship restricted to what part of
            the body is held at the Bentley Brook Inn in Ashbourne,
            Derbyshire?

   b.   Won in 2009 and again in 2010 by Taisto Miettinen and
            Kristiina Haapanen, which championships are run on a
            253.5-metre track in Sonkajärvi in Finland?

   c.   In the hybrid sport originally conceived by the French
            graphic artist Enki Bilal, four-minute rounds of what
            game alternate with three-minute bouts of boxing?

17 What adjective links a large autonomous region
in northern China; islands such as Islay, Jura and
Skye; one of the Inns of Court; and the part of the
ear that contains organs of the senses of hearing and
equilibrium?

Three bonus questions on glue

   a.   What term is the Greek word for 'glue', and denotes the
            billions of cells in the human brain that have neither
            axons nor dendrites, but pack the nerve cells together,
            covering everything except the synapses?

b. In quantum chromodynamics, the eight massless vector bosons known as 'gluons', because they 'glue' quarks together to form hadrons, are carriers or mediators of which fundamental force?

c. From the Latin meaning 'cause to adhere', what adjective describes a language in which word formation typically involves the joining together of linear sequences of morphemes, rather than inflexion?

18 In chemistry, muriate salts are the result of the reaction of which acid, formerly known as muriatic acid, with an inorganic or organic base?

Three bonus questions on a shared name element

a. John Nash, Edward Blore and Aston Webb were the three principal architects who rebuilt and restored which royal residence, first acquired by George the Third in 1761?

b. Buckfast Abbey, a Benedictine abbey founded in 1018, lies at the edge of which national park?

c. Buckland Abbey near Plymouth was the home of which Elizabethan explorer? His 'drum', the subject of a poem by Sir Henry Newbolt, is on display there.

19 The German Ritter, the Spanish Caballero and the French Chevalier are equivalent to what rank in Britain?

Three bonus questions on men born in 1770. In each case, name the person from his works.

a. *The Phenomenology of Spirit* and *The Science of Logic* are among the works of which German philosopher?

b. Known as 'the Ettrick shepherd', which Scottish literary figure wrote *The Private Memoirs and Confessions of a Justified Sinner* and *Scottish Pastorals, Poems, Songs, etc.*?

c. Which composer's work includes the 'Emperor' piano concerto and the 'Egmont' overture?

20 The oncoviruses, lentiviruses and foamy viruses belong to which family of enveloped, single-stranded RNA viruses? They all possess the enzyme reverse transcriptase, which allows integration of pro-viral DNA into the host genome.

Three bonus questions on a sport

a. Which Olympic sport is played in an area where the goals are three metres wide and only ninety centimetres high, and in which the two seven-a-side teams are distinguished by the colour of their caps?

b. In the 1956 Olympics, a water polo semi-final was stopped after a Soviet player inflicted a serious injury on an opponent from which country, in which the USSR had suppressed a revolt only weeks earlier?

c. What name, suggesting a kitchen implement, is given to a method of treading water used by water polo players to keep them upright and stable in the water?

21 Which contemporary arts centre in Bristol takes its name from a double portrait of 1434 by Jan van Eyck?

Three bonus questions on homophones. In each case, give the town whose name is the homophone of the word defined. For example, 'historic Cheshire town' and 'part of a yacht' is 'sale'. Got it?

a. A town in west Cornwall, and a variety of precipitation?

b. A river port in east Yorkshire, and a demon that preys on corpses or a person who delights in the macabre?

c. A town on the River Thames near Slough, and the past participle of a verb meaning 'destroy by corrosion', 'devour' or 'consume'?

22 The Russian doctor Michael Ostrog, the schoolmaster and barrister Montague John Druitt, the artist Walter Sickert and Prince Albert Victor, the Duke of Clarence, are among the men who have been suspected of being which infamous figure?

Three bonus questions on birds in poetry

a. To which bird does Wordsworth address the lines: 'There is madness about thee, and joy divine / In that song of thine'?

b. Which bird is the title and subject of a collection of poems by Ted Hughes, and is described at one point as being 'spraddled head-down in the beach-garbage, guzzling a / dropped ice-cream'?

c. What birds are being described by W.B. Yeats in the lines: 'All Suddenly mount / And scatter wheeling in great broken rings / Upon their clamorous wings'?

23 Three alumni of both Harvard University and its long-running humorous periodical were the founders in 1970 of which US magazine, noted for its parodies? It ceased publication in 1998.

Three bonus questions on Nobel laureates. In each case, I will give you the name of the first woman to win the Nobel Prize in a specific field. For five points each, name the prize and the decade in which they won it.

a. Bertha von Suttner?

b. Gerty Teresa Cori?

    c.   Elinor Ostrom?

 Located near Alum Bay, which series of chalk stacks forms the westernmost point of the Isle of Wight?

Three bonus questions on Italian buildings

    a.   The extensive monument in Rome's Piazza Venezia, known locally as 'the Wedding Cake' or 'the Typewriter', is dedicated to which Italian monarch?

    b.   Victor Emmanuel the Second is buried in which Roman building, also the last resting place of the artists Raphael and Annibale Carracci?

    c.   The four-storey arcade or galleria named after Victor Emmanuel the Second, designed by Guiseppe Mengoni and completed in 1877, is in which Italian city?

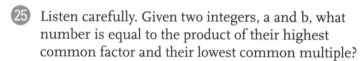 Listen carefully. Given two integers, a and b, what number is equal to the product of their highest common factor and their lowest common multiple?

Three bonus questions on pioneering female scientists

    a.   Born in 1706, Emilie du Châtelet was a scientist whose achievements included the first French translation of which work of 1687 by Newton, usually known by a single Latin word?

    b.   What was the surname of the woman thought to have been the first to receive a salary for scientific work? The sister of a private astronomer to George the Third, her own achievements include the discovery of several comets and nebulae.

    c.   Which Oxford college is named after the mathematician who wrote the influential 1834 work *On the Connexion of the Physical Sciences*?

26 In fluid dynamics, the Rayleigh-Taylor instability occurs at the interface of two fluids differing in what property?

Three bonus questions on physics

a. Respectively singular and plural, what shape characterises two different optical effects named after Einstein and Newton?

b. Newton's Rings, which can be seen when a convex lens is placed on a flat surface, are produced by what basic phenomenon of wave mechanics?

c. An Einstein ring is a distorted image of a distant astronomical source, produced by an effect known by what two-word name?

27 Meanings of what hyphenated alliterative word include a bi-stable electronic circuit capable of serving as one bit of memory, and a North American term for a backward somersault?

Three bonus questions on comedy at the Edinburgh Fringe

a. Winners of the main Perrier comedy award in 1997, which four-man group described themselves as a 'sketch-based team specialising in black comedy, and definitely not Oxbridge'?

b. Described by one reviewer as a 'faffer of real eloquence', which Irish comedian won the 2008 'If Comedy' award for his show *Let's Comedy* (sic), an act he described as 'basically, man faffs while light points. Plus chair'?

c. Describing her stage persona as an 'alley cat with delusions of grandeur', which comedienne was in 1995 the first female solo act to win the main Perrier award with a show entitled *Prozac and Tantrums*?

In physiology, what type of lymphocyte is the main agent of cell-mediated immunity? They are produced in bone marrow, migrate to the thymus to mature, and circulate between lymph nodes and bloodstream.

Three bonus questions on metabolic pathways

a. Which pathway converts glucose to pyruvate with the production of two molecules of ATP and two molecules of NADH for each glucose molecule processed?

b. Which pathway proceeds via five carbon intermediates and generates most cellular NADPH?

c. Which acid is produced in muscles during heavy exercise by the anaerobic conversion of pyruvate?

 Regarded as a major aspect of Portuguese architecture, what form of decorative item is an *azulejo*?

Three bonus questions on the decorative arts

a. His works including a five-metre-high sculpture under the dome of the main entrance to the V&A museum, the American artist Dale Chihuly works principally in what medium?

b. Which island in the Venetian lagoon gives its name to the decorative glass produced there since the end of the thirteenth century, when glassblowers were required to relocate from Venice to reduce the fire risk to the city?

c. Including glass doors, panelling, a font and an altar cross created in the Art Deco style by René Lalique, 'the glass church' of St Matthew's Church is at Millbrook on which island?

30 What two-word term describes an economic system containing both private and state enterprises?

Three bonus questions on German states

a. Wartburg Castle, where Martin Luther translated the New Testament from Latin into German in 1522, overlooks the city of Eisenach in which of Germany's sixteen modern states?

b. Which of the sixteen modern states was the only one to join the Federal Republic between its formation in 1949 and the reunification of Germany in 1990?

c. Following unification, Germany's three Stadts-Staaten or 'city states' are Berlin, Bremen and which other?

The Answers

1 Bourbon
- **a.** 1789
- **b.** 1793
- **c.** 1794

2 John Major
- **a.** Tephra
- **b.** Tuff
- **c.** Pyroclastic flow or pyroclastic density current (Greek: pur, 'fire'; klastos, 'broken in pieces')

3 Leviticus (Genesis, Exodus, Leviticus, Numbers and Deuteronomy)
- **a.** (RMS) *Titanic*
- **b.** *Speedwell*
- **c.** (RMS) *Mauretania*

4 Japan
- **a.** 78,770 km^2 (accept 73,7700–83,770 km^2)
- **b.** South Carolina (82,000 km^2; next closest are Virginia, 110,000 km^2 and Maryland, 32,000 km^2)
- **c.** Czech Republic (78,865 km^2; Austria, 83,000 km^2; Hungary, 93,000 km^2; Slovakia 49,000 km^2)

5 El (Salvador, Paso, Dorado)
- **a.** Tunisia
- **b.** Hokkaido
- **c.** Oman (parts of the UAE lie on the Strait, but this does not fit the question)

6 Los Angeles
- **a.** Ulster Cycle (accept but qualify Cuchulainn Cycle)
- **b.** W. B. Yeats
- **c.** Finn MacCool

7 Spreadsheet (not 'Excel', of course; it ran on Apple II computers)
- **a.** Star anise (star fruit is different, the fruit of the carambola)
- **b.** Galangal
- **c.** Turmeric

8 (Fallacy of the) Undistributed Middle
- **a.** Desire
- **b.** Symposium
- **c.** (René) Descartes

9 i-n-g-e-r (singer, finger, ginger)
- **a.** Lust / carnal sin
- **b.** Cerberus
- **c.** Dis ('la città infuocata di Dite', 'the burning city of Dis')

10 Council of Europe
- **a.** Orange gelato
- **b.** Steamed edamame
- **c.** Mushroom omelette

11 Secret (as in 'Scripture', 'History' and 'Garden')
- **a.** Andrew Motion ('A Song for Jonny [Wilkinson]', 2004)
- **b.** Sylvia Plath ('Daddy', written in 1963)
- **c.** George Orwell (*Nineteen Eighty-Four*, 1949)

12 Via (Bolivia and Latvia)
- **a.** (Republic of) Gabon
- **b.** Manganese
- **c.** Gulf of Guinea

13 Churchill (Lord Randolph and Sir Winston, both on 24 January)
- **a.** Sea cucumbers
- **b.** Sea gooseberries
- **c.** Sea anemones

14 Hydrazine / diazane
- **a.** Blue (an azure blue in the case of selenium)
- **b.** Calcium
- **c.** Potassium

15 Aspiration (not 'aspirate', 'aspirant' or 'aspire', of course, as these do not fit both clues)
- **a.** Stomach and spinach (hence the culinary expression 'Florentine')
- **b.** Protein and Frankenstein
- **c.** Quatrain and Captain

16 (Summer) Youth Olympics / (Summer Youth Olympic Games (not Junior Olympics)
- **a.** The toes (the World Toe Wrestling Championship)
- **b.** World Wife Carrying Championships
- **c.** Chess (specifically speed chess; the sport of chessboxing)

17 Inner (Inner Mongolia, Inner Hebrides, Inner Temple and inner ear)
- **a.** Glia (accept glial cells; accept but correct neuroglia)
- **b.** Strong (force; accept strong interaction, strong nuclear force, colour force)
- **c.** Agglutinative (accept agglutinate, agglutinating, correcting it)

18 Hydrochloric acid
- **a.** Buckingham Palace
- **b.** Dartmoor
- **c.** Sir Francis Drake

19 Knight
    a. (Georg Wilhelm Friedrich) Hegel
    b. (James) Hogg
    c. (Ludwig van) Beethoven

20 Retroviruses / *retroviridae*
    a. Water polo
    b. Hungary
    c. Eggbeater

21 Arnolfini (from *The Arnolfini Marriage*)
    a. Hayle / hail
    b. Goole / ghoul
    c. Eton / eaten

22 Jack the Ripper
    a. Skylark (accept but qualify lark; from 'To a Skylark')
    b. Crow
    c. (Wild) Swans ('The Wild Swans at Coole', from the title poem of the collection of the same title)

23 *National Lampoon* (a spin-off from *Harvard Lampoon*)
    a. Peace, 1900–1910 (1905; Austrian pacifist, author of *Lay Down Your Arms*)
    b. Medicine, 1940s (strictly Physiology or Medicine; 1948; work on the breakdown of glycogen; the Cori cycle)
    c. Economics, 2000–2010 (2009; for her analysis of economic governance)

24 The Needles
    a. Victor Emmanuel the Second
    b. The Pantheon
    c. Milan

25 A times b (accept ab or a multiplied by b)
    a. *Principia* (*Philosophiæ Naturalis Principia Mathematica*)

b. Herschel (Caroline Lucretia) (sister of William)
c. Somerville College (Mary Fairfax Somerville)

26 Density (density is defined as mass per unit volume)
a. Ring / rings
b. Interference
c. Gravitational lensing (i.e. by the bending of light by matter between source and observer)

27 Flip-flop
a. The League of Gentlemen (Jeremy Dyson, Mark Gatiss, Steve Pemberton and Reece Sheersmith)
b. David O'Doherty
c. Jenny Eclair (Emma Thompson and Penny Dwyer won as part of the Cambridge Footlights in 1981)

28 T cells / T lymphocytes
a. Embden-Meyerhof (Parnas) pathway or EMP pathway / glycolytic pathway / glycolysis
b. Pentose phosphate pathway (accept hexose monophosphate shunt or phospho-gluconate pathway)
c. Lactic acid / lactate

29 (Glazed, coloured, blue ceramic) Tile
a. Glass
b. Murano
c. Jersey

30 Mixed economy
a. Thuringia (Thuringen in German)
b. Saarland
c. Hamburg

Match Eleven

1 The idiosyncratic metre known as 'sprung rhythm' is especially associated with which poet? Received into the Roman Catholic church in 1866, his works include 'The Wreck of the Deutschland' and 'Pied Beauty'.

Three bonus questions on a literary character

a. 'There is no such thing as a moral or an immoral book. Books are well written, or badly written. That is all.' In the preface to which work of 1890 does the author make this assertion?

b. Entitled *Dorian: An Imitation*, which author's novel of 2003 transposes the character from the late nineteenth to the late twentieth century, and draws parallels between him and Princess Diana?

c. Which British choreographer also reworked and updated Wilde's novel, making Dorian a model for an advertising campaign, in a work which premiered at the 2008 Edinburgh Festival?

2 Listen carefully. In 1901, the first Nobel Prizes were awarded for achievements in five fields. In which field did the Bank of Sweden launch a sixth Nobel in 1969?

Three bonus questions on rivers

a. If the Mississippi and its tributary the Missouri are considered to be two separate rivers, which is the longest river in the world to flow through only one sovereign state?

b. Which is the only river that flows from the Alps to the North Sea?

c. What is the longest river in Europe west of Poland that flows through only one country?

3 What term describes the temperature below which water vapour in a volume of air precipitates out and, when the droplets are small enough, remains in suspension in the air to form a mist?

Three bonus questions on a science

a. Which field of science most commonly uses the sverdrup, a unit of fluid flow equal to one million cubic metres per second?

b. With an ultimate flow rate of up to 150 sverdrups, which warm ocean current enters the Atlantic through the straits of Florida at around 30 sverdrups?

c. A global system of ocean currents called the thermohaline circulation is driven by differences in temperature and in the concentration of what constituent of seawater?

4 What name did Edouard Manet give to his controversial 1863 portrait of Victorine Meurent, painted naked and reclining on her bed, save for a single slipper and a black ribbon at her throat?

Three bonus questions on a shared word element

a. From the Latin name of a forest deity, what adjective is used poetically for something associated with, or characteristic of, woods and woodland?

b. Named after a seventeenth-century anatomist, the deep lateral Sylvian fissure is found in which part of the human body?

c. The family of passerine birds with the scientific name *Sylvidae* has what common name, after their song? Species include Willow, Reed and Dartford.

5 Quote: 'You see in me the chief minister of police in Europe. I keep an eye on everything. My contacts are such that nothing escapes me.' These are the words of which Austrian statesman, who was head of government from 1815 to 1848?

Three bonus questions on the historical provinces of Japan, which were replaced by the current prefectures in the late nineteenth century

a. Comprising the modern Kochi prefecture on the island of Shikoku, which former province of Japan gives its name to a breed of mastiff originally bred for fighting?

b. Which province corresponds to the area of the former capital of Nara, and gives its name to the dominant ethnic group in Japan, as well as to a traditional style of painting and a Second World War battleship?

c. Comprising the south-west peninsula of the island of Kyushu, which former province gives its name to a variety of citrus fruit?

6 'I suppose the body to be just a statue or a machine made of earth.' Which French philosopher made this statement in the 1633 work *Treatise on Man*?

Three bonus questions on a French moralist

a. 'The height of cleverness is being able to conceal it.' This is one of the 'maxims' of which seventeenth-century French moralist, noted for his insights into the part that self-interest plays in human motivation?

b. What did La Rochefoucauld describe as 'a tribute that vice plays to virtue'?

c. 'Her novels are the maxims of La Rochefoucauld set in motion.' These words of the Italian novelist Di Lampedusa refer to which English author, born in 1775?

7 Give your full answer promptly for this. Four US states have names that end with the letters '-nia'; for ten points, name three of them.

Three bonus questions on a planetary system

a. Which planet was discovered in 1846 as a result of mathematical predictions made by Urbain le Verrier and John Couch Adams?

b. What is the largest moon of Neptune, named after the son of Poseidon in Greek mythology?

c. What is the second-largest Neptunian satellite? It shares its name with a shape-shifting Greek sea god.

8 First coined by Matt Stum on a 'Stash Hunt' mailing list in 2000, what term describes a real-world outdoor treasure-hunting hobby in which players try to locate hidden containers using GPS-enabled devices?

Three bonus questions on mononyms, or people known by single names

a. In 1718, shortly after his release from the Bastille on charges of writing satirical verses about the Regent, the writer and philosopher François-Marie Arouet adopted what name?

b. With the first names Sidonie-Gabrielle, which French writer, whose first book appeared in 1900, became known by her surname which she adopted as her penname?

   c. Born in 1783, the French novelist Marie-Henri Beyle wrote *The Red and the Black* and *The Charterhouse at Parma* under what mononym, adapted from the name of a Prussian town?

9 Which US-Canadian singer-songwriter made his debut as a composer of opera in 2009 with *Prima Donna*, having previously released albums including *Want One* and *Poses*?

Three bonus questions on love triangles in literature. In each case, I want the name of the third member of the triangle.

   a. Quasimodo, Captain Phoebus and...?

   b. Jay Gatsby, Tom Buchanan and...?

   c. Mr Wickham, Mr Darcy and...?

10 In 1811, which chemist first proposed the statement that equal volumes of gases at the same temperature and pressure contain the same numbers of molecules?

Three bonus questions on scientific apparatus

   a. Born in 1791, which British scientist gives his name to an enclosure of conducting material that protects electronic equipment from electrostatic discharges?

   b. Derived from that of the botanist who devised it in around 1829, what name was given to a glass case used to house plants, particularly ferns, both domestically and during transportation from overseas?

   c. The father of a noted novelist, which nineteenth-century engineer gives his name to a shield or screen which houses meteorological instruments whilst allowing the free circulation of air around them?

11 First performed in 1850 and 1882, which two operas by Richard Wagner bear the names of a son and his father?

Three bonus questions on the arts

a. A mural called the *Beethoven Frieze* and the painting *Frau Adele Bloch-Bauer* are twentieth-century works by which Austrian artist?

b. The works of which Austrian novelist include *Young Törless* in 1906, and the long modernist novel *The Man Without Qualities*, left unfinished on his death in 1942?

c. *Resurrection Symphony*, *Ode to Heavenly Joy* and *Symphony of a Thousand* are popular names for orchestral works by which composer, who died in Vienna in 1911?

12 Which island country in Asia is named after the King of Spain who married Mary the First of England in 1554?

Three bonus questions on English kings

a. Which English king, also known as Edward of Caernarvon, was defeated by the Scots at Bannockburn in 1314?

b. At which decisive battle in Gloucestershire in 1471 did Edward the Fourth defeat the Lancastrians to reclaim his throne?

c. In August 1346, at which battle of the Hundred Years War did Edward the Third and his son Edward the Black Prince defeat the French with a force that included several thousand longbowmen?

13 What informal term is commonly used for the economic and monetary union of nineteen European Union member states that have adopted a common currency as their sole legal tender?

Three bonus questions on a shared prefix

a. Its name having the same Latin source as the adjective 'ebullient', an ebulliometer is a device used in physics to determine what quality of a solution?

b. Ebullioscopy is a technique for finding what quantity of a substance by means of measuring the extent to which it elevates the boiling point of a suitable solvent?

c. In the phenomenon called ebullism, what is formed in body fluids as a result of greatly reduced barometric pressure?

14 Particularly associated with oil exploration in the late nineteenth and early twentieth centuries, what term indicates the situation that occurs in a well when the formation pressure exceeds the pressure applied to it by the column of drilling fluid, resulting in an uncontrolled flow of crude oil?

Three bonus questions on authors who died in 2010. In each case, identify the person from the description.

a. A Liverpool-born novelist, her works include *Young Adolf*, *An Awfully Big Adventure* and *Master Georgie*?

b. The historian and political commentator whose works include *Ill Fares the Land*, *The Memory Chalet* and *Postwar: A History of Europe since 1945*?

c. A sporting figure who became a bestselling author of genre fiction, his works include *Dead Cert*, *Whip Hand* and *Under Orders*?

15 The tusks of elephants are elongated teeth that grow continuously at about 20 centimetres a year. Which teeth are modified to form elephant tusks?

Three bonus questions on the *Iliad*

a. In the opening lines of the *Iliad*, the poet invokes the goddess to sing of the 'cursed anger' of which Greek hero?

b. Later in the *Iliad*, whose death causes Achilles to say, 'I will make these Trojan women and deep-bosomed daughters of Dardanus wipe the tears from their tender cheeks with both their hands to raise the dirge'?

c. Who is the mother of Achilles, who preserves the body of Patroclus from decay and gives her son the armour made for him by Vulcan?

16 In probability theory, what name is given to the theorem stating that the mean value of a sequence of trials approaches the expected value, as the number of trials increases?

Three bonus questions on cheese making

a. What enzyme, traditionally derived from the stomach of a mammal, is used to coagulate casein in the initial stage of making hard cheese?

b. Species of which genus of fungi are responsible for the veins in blue cheeses such as Stilton and Roquefort?

c. The production of carbon dioxide by *Proprionibacterium freudenreichii* is responsible for a characteristic of the appearance of which Swiss cheese?

17 Which year saw the discovery of nuclear fission by Hahn and Strassman, the publication of Graham Greene's *Brighton Rock*, the first coverage of the Boat Race by BBC Television, and the annexation of Austria by the Third Reich?

Three bonus questions on Egyptian gods

a. In Egyptian mythology, Amon is the creator of the world and Ra maintains it by means of the passage of the Sun. Who created man and gave him wisdom?

b. Which god of wisdom invented writing and was the protector of Egyptian officials, meaning that he was responsible for the efficient running of the state?

c. After the world was created, which god became king of Egypt and ruled together with his sister-consort Isis?

18 What five-letter acronym denotes the government's central database system which aims to show how much is spent by each government department and each spending programme?

Three bonus questions on events of the 1990s

a. Which republic marked the twentieth anniversary of its unification on 22 May 2010?

b. A so-called unification flag was first used in 1991 at the World Table Tennis Championships and the World Youth Football Championships; both occasions saw which two countries competing as a single team?

c. Which country holds an annual national holiday on 3 October, celebrating its reunification on that date in 1990?

19 In medicine, the term 'sternutation' denotes an attack of what?

Three bonus questions on deaths attributed to laughter

a. Said to have died in a fit of laughter around 206 BC after watching a donkey eat figs, Chrysippus of Soli was, along with Zeno and Cleanthes, a leading figure in which school of philosophy?

b. Last in the line of Wilfred the Hairy of Barcelona, Martin the Humanist is thought to have died of a combination of uncontrollable laughter and serious indigestion. Of which Spanish kingdom did he become ruler in 1396?

c. A Scottish scholar and translator who lost his collection of manuscripts after the Battle of Worcester, Sir Thomas Urquhart is said to have died 'in a fit of mirth' on hearing of the succession of which king, whose cause he had supported?

20 What adjective denotes: in geometry, the angle opposite the base of a triangle; in music, the relationship of notes sounded together; and, in medicine, the transmission of disease genetically, congenitally or perinatally?

Three bonus questions on pairs of words whose spelling differs by the addition of a 't' at the beginning, for example 'rash' and 'trash'. In each case, give both words from the definitions.

a. 'To turn over and over on an axis' and 'one who tries to disrupt an internet community by provocative posts or messages'?

b. 'Of great vertical extent' and 'location of the semitendinosus muscle'?

c. 'Handsome, muscular man' and 'dull, abrupt sound'?

21 Answer as soon as you buzz. Multiply the number of platonic solids by the number of faces on the most multifaceted among them. What three-digit number results?

Three bonus questions on spirals

a. A spiral with the polar equation r equals a theta is usually named after which Greek mathematician?

b. What name is given to a spiral in which the length of the radius vector is inversely proportional to its angle with the polar axis, so that its equation is r theta equals a?

c. Which Swiss mathematician investigated the logarithmic spiral, which he called the 'spira mirabilis', and requested that one be carved on his tomb, although following his death in 1705 an Archimedian spiral was inscribed instead?

22 In sociology, what two-word term describes the hierarchical arrangement of individuals according to wealth, status and power that was deemed necessary by such functionalists as Talcott Parsons?

Three bonus questions on social sciences

a. Used in the subtitle of a 1985 work by the US sociologists Rodney Stark and William Sims Bainbridge, what term denotes the process by which religious institutions, beliefs and practices lose their social significance?

b. Coined by the US sociologist Harold Garfinkel, what term describes the study of the methods by which individuals accomplish their daily actions and make sense of their social world?

    c.   Explored by Homi K. Bhabha as a legacy of colonialism, what is the process by which individuals and social groups are made peripheral to the mainstream by relegating them to the outer edges of society?

23 In March 1950, Thomas Holden became the first person to be placed officially on which list, in a programme implemented by J. Edgar Hoover?

Three bonus questions on a position

    a.   What role or position is offered to the homeless Davies by Aston and Mick in the three-character play of 1960 by Harold Pinter, the position also being the play's title?

    b.   In November 1834, while Sir Robert Peel was in Italy, which former Prime Minister led a caretaker government with himself as Home, Foreign and Colonial secretary?

    c.   Joe Mercer, Howard Wilkinson and Peter Taylor have all held what post as caretakers?

24 Deriving from the Latin, what term is used for air or other gases that have been thinned or have had their density reduced, and is used figuratively for anything considered particularly fine or exalted?

Three bonus questions on things 'rare'

    a.   'Rare earths' is a term sometimes applied to the series of elements in the periodic table usually known by what name, derived from the element with atomic number 57?

    b.   'Rare bird', a phrase denoting something exceptional or extraordinary, derives from the phrase 'rara avis' in the satires of which Roman author?

    c.   'Rare Ben', the word in this case meaning 'remarkable', is part of the inscription on the tomb in Westminster Abbey of which dramatist, who died in 1637?

25 Listen carefully. What is the present name of the English city whose Roman name is an anagram of the television channel formerly known as UKTV G2 and renamed because, allegedly, 'Everyone knows a bloke [of this name]'?

Three bonus questions on an ancient city

a. Which city was a Roman colony under Julius Caesar, is known for St Paul's letters to its people, and has given its name to one of the classical orders of architecture?

b. The Isthmus of Corinth joins the Peloponnese to mainland Greece and separates the Saronic Gulf, an inlet of the Aegean sea, from the Gulf of Corinth, an inlet of which sea?

c. Which naval battle of 1571 was a victory for the Holy League over the Ottoman Empire, and took place between the Gulf of Corinth and the Gulf of Patras?

26 What adjective links two-word terms meaning: in chemistry, ethanol that contains less than one per cent of water by weight; in politics, a majority over all rivals combined; and, in physics, the lowest temperature that is theoretically possible?

Three bonus questions on twentieth-century fashion firsts

a. Dating to antiquity and used by women in the USA from the late nineteenth century as a sign of social non-conformity, what product was marketed for the first time from 1915 in the now-familiar containers devised by the US cosmetician Maurice Levy?

b. Commissioned by a French couturier, which enduring product was created in 1921 by Ernest Beaux?

c.   In 1960, the Warner's lingerie company introduced the
     'Little Godiva Step-in Girdle', believed to be the first
     garment made of which synthetic polyurethane fibre
     with the elastic properties of rubber?

27 Which decade saw the publication of George Eliot's
Middlemarch and Tolstoy's *Anna Karenina*, the
first performance of Bizet's *Carmen*, and the first
Impressionist exhibition in Paris?

Three bonus questions on deaths in the novels of E.M. Forster

a.   In which novel by Forster did the high number of deaths
     lead one critic to calculate that there is a forty-four
     per cent mortality rate among the adult characters? An
     accident in a football game and a fatal encounter with
     a train are two of the methods he uses to dispatch his
     characters.

b.   'A stick, very bright, descended. It hurt him, not where
     it descended, but in the heart. Books fell over him in
     a shower. Nothing had sense.' In which novel does
     Forster use these words to describe the last moments of
     Leonard Bast?

c.   'Nothing ever happens to me,' reflects the heroine
     of which of Forster's novels, just minutes before she
     witnesses a violent death in Florence's Piazza Signoria?

28 Often used disparagingly, what term is the trademark
name of the system developed by the US inventor
Major General George O. Squier in 1922 to transmit
recorded music to public places?

Three bonus questions on circumlocutions

a. To what specific weather phenomenon was the US Environmental Protection Agency referring when it used the phrase 'poorly buffered precipitation'?

b. 'User friendly, space effective, flexible deskside sortation units', an expression devised by an agency of the Canadian government, means what in everyday English?

c. What did a leading telecoms company mean when it reported in 2008 that around 1,800 employees in Finland had been affected by 'synergy-related headcount restructuring'?

29 *Thoughts on Lotteries, The Life and Morals of Jesus of Nazareth* and *Notes on the State of Virginia* are among the writings of which political figure, the third President of the United States of America?

Three bonus questions on red hair

a. 'You'd find it easier to be bad than good if you had red hair ... people who haven't red hair don't know what trouble is.' In which novel of 1908 do these words appear?

b. 'Ethiopians say that their gods are snub-nosed and black, Thracians that theirs are pale and red-haired.' These words are attributed to which pre-Socratic philosopher, a native of Colophon in Ionia?

c. 'Out of the ash / I rise with my red hair / And I eat men like air.' These are the final words of 'Lady Lazarus', a work by which poet who died in 1963?

30 Which US manufacturer's aircraft include the P-38 Lightning, the C-130 Hercules, the L-049 Constellation and the F-117a Stealth Fighter?

Three bonus questions on the states of Brazil

a. The states of Paraná, Santa Caterina and Rio Grande do Sul all share borders with which country?

b. The states of Acre, Mato Grosso and Rondonia all border which country?

c. For five points, name two of the three countries with which the state of Amazonas shares borders?

The Answers

1 (Gerard Manley) Hopkins
    a. *The Picture of Dorian Gray* (accept 'The Portrait of...', correcting it)
    b. Will Self
    c. Matthew Bourne (*Dorian Gray*)

2 Economics
    a. Yangtze / Chang Jiang (the Nile, Amazon and Irtysh all flow through more than one country)
    b. Rhine
    c. Loire

3 Dew point / saturation temperature / point of saturation / condensation point (larger droplets are deposited on the ground as dew)
    a. Oceanography (after Harald Ulrik Sverdrup)
    b. Gulf Stream
    c. Salt

4 *Olympia*
    a. Sylvan (from Silvanus)
    b. Cerebrum (accept 'brain')
    c. Warbler

5 (Prince Clemens) Metternich
    a. Tosa
    b. Yamato
    c. Satsuma

6 (René) Descartes
- **a.** (François Duc de) la Rochefoucauld
- **b.** Hypocrisy
- **c.** (Jane) Austen

7 California, Pennsylvania, Virginia, West Virginia
- **a.** Neptune
- **b.** Triton
- **c.** Proteus

8 Geocaching
- **a.** Voltaire
- **b.** Colette (her first four novels appeared under her husband's penname, 'Willy')
- **c.** Stendhal (from Stendal)

9 Rufus Wainwright
- **a.** Esmeralda (in *Notre Dame de Paris* by Hugo)
- **b.** Daisy (Buchanan, née Fay; in *The Great Gatsby* by Fitzgerald)
- **c.** Elizabeth (Bennett; in *Pride and Prejudice* by Austen)

10 (Amedeo) Avogadro
- **a.** Michael Faraday (the Faraday cage / box / shield)
- **b.** Wardian case (Dr Nathaniel Bagshaw Ward)
- **c.** (Thomas) Stevenson (father of Robert Louis; the Stevenson screen)

11 Lohengrin and Parsifal
- **a.** (Gustav) Klimt
- **b.** (Robert) Musil
- **c.** (Gustav) Mahler

12 The Philippines (Philip the Second of Spain)
- **a.** Edward the Second
- **b.** Tewkesbury

    c.   Crécy

13 Eurozone (accept but qualify Euroland)
    a.   (True) Boiling point
    b.   Molecular weight (accept [relative] molecular mass)
    c.   (Gas) Bubbles

14 Blowout / gusher (accept wild well)
    a.   Beryl Bainbridge (1913–2010)
    b.   Tony Judt (1948–2010)
    c.   Dick Francis (1920–2010)

15 Incisors (specifically second incisors of the upper jaw)
    a.   Achilles ('Achilles' cursed anger sing, o goddess'; Pope's translation)
    b.   Patroclus
    c.   Thetis

16 (Strong / Weak) Law of Large Numbers (also known as LLN)
    a.   Rennin, chymosin (allow rennet)
    b.   *Penicillium*
    c.   Emmental(er)

17 1938
    a.   Ptah
    b.   Thoth / Thot
    c.   Osiris

18 COINS (Combined Online Information System)
    a.   Yemen
    b.   North Korea and South Korea
    c.   Germany

19 Sneezing
    a.   Stoics / Stoicism
    b.   Aragon

    c.   Charles the Second

20 Vertical
    a.   Roll and troll
    b.   High and thigh
    c.   Hunk and thunk

21 100 (5 platonic solids x 20 faces on an icosahedron)
    a.   Archimedes
    b.   Hyperbolic (or reciprocal) spiral
    c.   Jacob (or James or Jacques) Bernoulli

22 Social stratification (do not accept 'class system')
    a.   'Secularization' (*The Future of Religion: Secularization, Revival and Cult Formation*)
    b.   Ethnomethodology
    c.   Marginalisation

23 'Most Wanted' (i.e. the FBI's ten most wanted fugitives)
    a.   (The) Caretaker
    b.   (Arthur Wellesley) Duke of Wellington
    c.   England football manager

24 Rarefied (Latin: *rarefacere*, 'grow thin' or 'become rare')
    a.   Lanthanides / lanthanoids
    b.   Juvenal
    c.   Ben Jonson

25 Chester (i.e. Deva from Dave)
    a.   Corinth
    b.   Ionian Sea
    c.   Battle of Lepanto

26 Absolute (alcohol, majority, zero)
    a.   Lipstick (i.e. in a push-up tube)
    b.   Chanel No. 5

    c.   Lycra (accept spandex; Lycra is a trade name for spandex)

㉗ 1870s (1871–1872; 1873–1877; 1875; 1874)
    a.   *The Longest Journey*
    b.   *Howard's End*
    c.   *A Room With a View*

㉘ Muzak (transmission over electrical lines without the use of radio)
    a.   Acid rain (prompt for more if they answer 'rain')
    b.   Wastepaper baskets
    c.   They were sacked

㉙ (Thomas) Jefferson
    a.   *Anne of Green Gables* (by L.M. Montgomery)
    b.   Xenophanes
    c.   Sylvia Plath

㉚ Lockheed (now Lockheed Martin)
    a.   Argentina (Paraná also borders Paraguay; Rio Grande do Sul also borders Uruguay)
    b.   Bolivia (Acre also borders Peru)
    c.   Peru, Colombia, Venezuela

Match Twelve

1 What adjective has been formed from the English name of the Chinese city of Guangzhou and has been applied to the city's inhabitants, its dialect, and its style of cooking?

Three bonus questions on a play by Shakespeare

a. The subject of which play by Shakespeare had, according to Plutarch, composed for himself a gravestone inscription that declared 'Here, having ended years of misery, I lie still. / Ask not my name, vile men, I wish you every ill'?

b. The title of which novel of 1962 by Vladimir Nabokov is taken from a line spoken in Act Four of *Timon of Athens*?

c. Which Canadian-born British Vorticist exhibited a series of illustrations in 1912, intended to accompany an edition of *Timon of Athens*?

2 What area of Stoke-on-Trent took its name from an ancient state of central Italy known for its artistic achievements, in reference to the re-establishment there in 1769 of the Wedgewood pottery business?

Three bonus questions on an Italian city

a. In 1300, Pope Boniface the Eighth paid tribute to the people of which city, declaring them to be the 'fifth element', alongside fire, water, earth and air?

b. Containing artwork by Donatello and Giotto, which Franciscan abbey in Florence is the burial place of, amongst others, Michelangelo, Galileo and Machiavelli?

c. In 2008, 700 years after it was issued, Florence's city council revoked a sentence declaring that which poet would be burned at the stake if he ever returned to the city?

3 What five-letter word is a contraction in informal use described by the *Oxford Dictionary of English* as 'a general-purpose "filler", being used in questions in colloquial speech or very informal writing both to seek confirmation or merely for emphasis'?

Three bonus questions on chess terminology

a. In chess, a deliberate sacrifice, usually of a pawn, in return for an advantage in position and development is known by what term?

b. What French term is spoken by a player to indicate that he or she intends to correct the position of a piece on the board without performing an actual move?

c. Along with a queen, which chess piece is considered to be a 'major piece'?

4 'Discovering [him] was like discovering where I lived ... It was, as Goethe described the experience of reading [him], like walking into a lighted room.' These words of the politician and broadcaster Bryan Magee refer to which German philosopher, born in 1724?

Three bonus questions on astronomy. I want you to identify each astronomer from his description in the 'Astronomers' Drinking Song', published in 1866 by the British mathematician Augustus de Morgan.

a. Which astronomer 'believed the Earth stood still, sir, / He never would have blundered so, / Had he but drunk his fill, sir'?

b. And who, 'placed the stars, / Each in its due location; / He lost his nose by spite of Mars, / But that was no privation'?

c. And who sings: 'Whate'er you think you prove, / The Earth must go its way, sirs; / Spite of your teeth I'll make it move, / For I'll drink my bottle a day, sirs'?

5 'The gift is mine, the choice is thine.' In 1932, the British publisher Harold Raymond used this slogan to launch which innovation, devised after he had received 119 Christmas presents, only three of which were books?

Three bonus questions on returning to power

a. Meaning the recovery or regaining of something lost, the term 'readeption' is usually applied to the return to the English throne of which king in 1470?

b. Jean-Bertrand Aristide became the first democratically elected President of which Caribbean country in 1990? Removed by a coup in 1991, he was restored to power, with US intervention, in 1994.

c. What name is popularly given to the period between March and June 1815, from Napoleon's resumption of power after his exile on Elba to his defeat at Waterloo?

6 Differing only in that one has an additional final letter, give both of the words which mean 'basic structural and functional unit of an organism', and 'string instrument for which Barber, Elgar and Boccherini all wrote concerti'?

Three bonus questions on pairs of words whose spelling differs by the addition of a 't' after the third letter, for example 'pin' and 'pint'. In each case, give both words from the definitions.

a. 'A pipe for conveying smoke or hot air', and 'a wind instrument'?

b. 'Lesson of a story or fable', and 'liable to death and, hence, ungodlike'?

c. 'Nerve cell', and 'uncharged particle of similar mass to a proton'?

7 Quote: 'A squeezing, wrenching, grasping, scraping, clutching, covetous old sinner! Hard and sharp as flint, from which no steel had ever struck out generous fire.' These words describe which character, the protagonist of a novella of 1843?

Three bonus questions on quotations

a. In Dickens' *Pickwick Papers*, Sam Weller says that 'poverty' and which shellfish 'always seem to go together'?

b. In which play by Arthur Miller does the central character, Willie Loman, say, 'The world is an oyster, but you don't crack it open on a mattress'?

c. Which Dublin-born satirist, under the pseudonym Simon Wagstaff, published *Polite and Ingenious Conversation* in 1738, which includes the line 'He was a bold man that first ate an oyster'?

8. Words meaning 'ungrateful person', 'Moroccan port on the Straits of Gibraltar' and 'act of ripping or rending' are all anagrams of the name of which igneous rock?

Three bonus questions on a word element

a. The marine snails of the family *Muricidae* exude a yellow fluid that, when exposed to sunlight, becomes a dye of what colour, associated with royalty in ancient times?

b. Which member of the *Muridae* family of rodents has species that include Flat-haired and Pygmy?

c. In plants, muriform cells are so-called because they are arranged regularly in a pattern that resembles what?

9. Hampton House, Belfast; Milburngate House, Durham; Old Hall Street, Liverpool; and 3 Northgate, Glasgow are four of the regional offices of which UK government service, which has its London office at Olympia house?

Three bonus questions on place names. All three answers begin with the same two letters.

a. One of the shallowest in the world, which sea is linked to the Black Sea by the Strait of Kerch?

b. What is the modern name of the village in the Pas de Calais that is the site of a battle of October 1415?

c. Which group of islands includes Graciosa, Pico and Sao Miguel?

10. Noted for an early statement of the principle of the conservation of energy, which German chemist, born in 1806, gives his name to a balance used to determine density by weighing a solid when suspended in air, and to the salt ferrous ammonium sulphate?

Three bonus questions on biochemistry

a. What element is present in a molecule of the amino acid glucosamine, but not in glucose?

b. Peptidoglycan in the cell walls of bacteria is a polymer of N-acetyl glucosamine and which other monosaccharide?

c. What polymer of glucosamine residues is the main component of the exoskeletons of crustaceans and the cell walls of fungi?

11 Used in anatomy for a cavity serving as an entrance to another, especially that of the nose or inner ear, what word is used more generally to mean an entrance hall?

Three bonus questions on animals

a. In January 1961, 'Ham' returned safely after being sent into space by the USA. What species was he?

b. In 1967, which primatologist became scientific director of the Gombe Research Institute in Tanzania, where she carried out a study of chimpanzees that demonstrated the complexity of primate behaviour?

c. James Lever was longlisted for the 2009 Man Booker Prize for his satire on the genre of the Hollywood memoir, in the form of the supposed autobiography of which chimpanzee?

12 The G6 economic forum of six countries was joined by Canada in 1976 and then by which other country in 1998 to form the G8?

Three bonus questions on the names of wars

a. The conflict often called the English Civil War is now sometimes given what name by historians, including Trevor Royle in the subtitle of his work of 2005, to take into account the simultaneous and subsequent fighting in Scotland and Ireland?

b. The 18th-century war called the Third Carnatic War in India, the French and Indian War in the USA, and the Third Silesian War in central Europe is known by what name in the UK?

c. Fought between Britain and Spain from 1739 to 1748, la Guerra del Asiento, meaning the War of the Contract, is known in English by what name?

13 Ending a record-breaking 541 days of political deadlock, December 2011 saw the swearing-in of a new government in which European country?

Three bonus questions on volcanos

a. Peléan eruptions are named after the 1902 eruption of Mont Pelée that devastated the town of St Pierre on which island in the Lesser Antilles?

b. Named after an Italian volcano, what type of eruption involves moderate bursts of expanding gases that eject clots of incandescent lava in small, cyclical eruptions?

c. Involving the explosive ejection of relatively viscous lava, the most powerful type of eruption is named after which Roman scholar, who died in AD 79?

14 In biology, what term is used for the space enclosed by an organ, such as the bladder, or a tubular structure, such as the gastrointestinal tract? The same word is the SI unit for the measure of the rate of flow of light.

Three bonus questions on a plant family

a. What is the common name for the *Poaceae*? They are generally regarded as the most significant plant family in terms of human economics, and include sugar cane and sorghum?

b. What name is given to the horizontal underground stems or rootstocks that send shoots above ground, a common means of reproduction in grasses?

c. What is the common name of the grass *Secale cereale*, which thrives in high altitudes, is grown as far north as the Arctic Circle, and is used to make bread and whisky?

15. One of three women awarded the Nobel Peace Prize in 2011, Ellen Johnson-Sirleaf became the first woman to be elected head of state in Africa when she was inaugurated as President of which West African country in 2006?

Three bonus questions on female Nobel laureates since 2000. In each case, give me the nationality of the recipient and the prize they won.

a. Shirin Ebadi?

b. Elfriede Jelinek?

c. Ada Yonath?

16. Narrated by the subject's servant *Tiro*, *Imperium* and *Lustrum* are the first and second novels in Robert Harris's trilogy about which Roman statesman, writer and orator?

Three bonus questions on a name

a. What word for a gentle breeze derives from the name given in Greek mythology to the personification of the west wind?

b. In one version of the Greek myth, Zephyrus and Apollo competed for the affections of which youth? Discovering that he preferred Apollo, Zephyrus killed him and from his spilled blood grew the flower named after him.

c. In July 2010, the UK-built *Zephyr*, described as the first 'eternal plane', broke the record for an unmanned aerial vehicle when it flew non-stop for over a week by what means of power?

17 The films *Can't Stop the Music, Howard the Duck, Cocktail, The Last Airbender* and *Battlefield Earth* have all been recipients of the Worst Picture award at which annual ceremony in Los Angeles?

Three bonus questions on the human condition

a. 'Experience declares that man is the only animal which devours his own kind; for I can apply no milder term ... to the general prey of the rich on the poor.' These are the words of which future US President, in a letter of 1787?

b. 'Man is the only creature that consumes without producing.' In which allegorical work of 1945 do these words appear?

c. 'Man is the only animal that blushes. Or needs to.' Which American humourist wrote these words in a work of 1897?

18 The Volta Bureau Research Library was founded in Washington DC in the 1880s by which Scottish-born scientist and inventor, with the Volta prize money awarded him by the French government?

Three bonus questions on a fibre

a. *Gossypium*, a plant in the mallow family, is the source of which fibre?

b. Similar devices having been used earlier in China and India, which machine was developed by the American Eli Whitney in 1793, for removing seeds from cotton fibres?

c. After the Victorian English chemist who devised it, what name is given to the chemical treatment of cotton with strong alkalis, to improve both strength and texture?

19 Listen carefully and answer as soon as you buzz. A car accelerates from rest at 10 metres per second squared for a period of five seconds. How far has it travelled?

Three bonus questions on two-dimensional shapes. In each case, I want the size of their symmetry group, that is, the number of rotations and reflections they possess in total – including the identity symmetry in which the shape is left unmoved.

a. The letter Z?

b. An equilateral triangle?

c. A regular octagon?

20 Naskh, Tulut and Muhaqqaq are among the cursive styles of the calligraphy of which language and alphabet?

Three bonus questions on languages

a. Thought to derive from a corruption of the word 'business', what term denotes a simplified language produced by contact between groups that have no common language?

b. Ultimately from the Latin for 'bring into being', what term denotes a pidgin that becomes the mother tongue of a community?

c. A creole reckoned to have more than a million first-language speakers, Tok Pisin is an official language of which commonwealth member state?

21 What three-word term denotes the meteorological event whose most severe period coincided with the Maunder Minimum of sunspot activity between 1645 and 1715?

Three bonus questions on national nature reserves

a. Threatened by a proposed tidal barrier, which national nature reserve in Lincolnshire and Norfolk is a mix of open and coastal water, mudflats and salt marshes?

b. Which Welsh mountain to the south east of Barmouth rises to 2,930 feet and is one of the most southerly limits of arctic alpine flora in Britain?

c. A Scottish nature reserve, which island is the location of Fingal's Cave, popularised by Mendelssohn's 'Hebrides Overture'?

22 'Gap', 'Day-Age', 'Old Earth' and 'Young Earth' are versions of what belief in the origin of life as it is described in the Book of Genesis?

Three bonus questions on an adjective

a. 'The Victorious' is the meaning of the Arabic name of which African city, referring to the arrival in 974 of the Fatimid Caliph al-Muizz, the city being established as the capital of the Caliphate?

b. The first active mission of the aircraft carrier HMS *Victorious* was an air strike of 24 May 1941 against which German battleship, which sank three days later?

  c. Which African president, who died in 2003, had awarded himself the VC, in this instance meaning 'Victorious Cross', and had appointed himself CBE, meaning 'Conqueror of the British Empire'?

23 In recognition of the role played by drama and poetry in its cultural life and, among other things, the quality and diversity of its publishing, which British city was the world's first UNESCO City of Literature, in 2004?

Three bonus questions on world cities

  a. The fortieth parallel of latitude passes through the cities of Philadelphia, Ankara and which East Asian capital?

  b. London and the Canadian city of Calgary both lie between the 51st and 52nd parallels. Which Central Asian capital is closest in latitude?

  c. Which capital of the Americas lies close to the same parallel of latitude as Venice and Zagreb?

24 The Belgian strip cartoonist Georges Remi used a phonetic version of his reversed initials to form which pseudonym?

Three bonus questions on poetry

  a. In a work of 1898, which poet writes that 'Each man kills the thing he loves ... The coward does it with a kiss, / The brave man with a sword'?

  b. 'No coward soul is mine, / No trembler in the world's storm-troubled sphere'; this couplet begins the 'Last Lines' of which author and poet, who died in 1848?

  c. 'Thus conscience doth make cowards of us all.' Which of Shakespeare's title characters says these words?

25 Which historical figure links a tragedy by Schiller, dramas by Jean Anouilh and George Bernard Shaw, and Voltaire's poem 'La Pucelle'? Born around 1412, she was finally canonised in 1920.

Three bonus questions on pilgrimage

a. The Pilgrims' Way, which runs along parts of the North Downs Way, follows the 120-mile pilgrimage route between Canterbury and which city?

b. The second-largest site of pilgrimage in France after Lourdes is the Basilica of Saint Thérèse in which town in Northern France?

c. Which so-called pilgrimage constituted a major Tudor rebellion in Northern England from 1536, against the policies and ministers of Henry the Eighth, led by Lord Darcy and Robert Aske?

26 From a Latin word meaning 'to begin', what term for the beginning of a project or undertaking provides the title of a film of 2010 directed by Christopher Nolan?

Three bonus questions on Europe. In each case, give the smallest European countries, by land area, in each of the following categories.

a. The smallest country bordering Germany?

b. The smallest country with a coastline on the Adriatic Sea?

c. The smallest European country on the Prime Meridian?

27 The name of which symbol of the French Republic is an anagram for an inhabitant of the West Asian country whose capital is Yerevan?

Three bonus questions on so-called 'cognate anagrams', that is, words that are both anagrams of and are suggested by the given word or phrase. For instance, 'moon starer' would give the single word answer 'astronomer'. Got it?

a. 'Enraged' has what anagram that resembles it in meaning?

b. The expression 'terminal cut' has what single-word 'cognate anagram'?

c. 'Lithe acts' is a cognate anagram of a single-word term for what activity?

28 You may answer this in Latin or English. Directed against Martin Luther, Henry the Eighth's treatise Defence of the Seven Sacraments is the origin of which inscription on British coins?

Three bonus questions on monarchs

a. What name and regnal number were shared by all the following: the first Bourbon King of France, the third Franconian or Salian Emperor of the Holy Roman Empire; and the first Lancastrian King of England?

b. What name and number were shared by two rulers, one in thirteenth-century Germany nicknamed 'Stupor Mundi' or 'the Wonder of the World', and the other, in eighteenth-century Prussia, called 'the Great'?

c. What name and regnal number were shared by the Duke of Edinburgh's grandfather and the Queen's great-great-great-great-great-great-grandfather?

29 Kurmanji and Sorani are among varieties of which Indo-European language? Lacking a homeland, its speakers are estimated at more than 15 million and are spread over eastern Turkey, Iran, Syria and Iraq.

Three bonus questions on Russian novelists

a. Which novelist was arrested in 1849 for being a member of a liberal intellectual group? After a mock execution, his death sentence was commuted to four years of penal servitude in Siberia.

b. In an obituary of the writer Nikolai Gogol, which author's praise of the deceased writer so incensed the authorities that he was sent to prison for a month before being exiled to his estate for nearly two years?

c. Which novelist spent eight years in prison for criticising Stalin? Awarded the Nobel Prize in 1971, he is noted for his exposure of the brutalities of the Soviet system.

30 Etymologically unrelated, meanings of what three-letter word include: a shrub with aromatic leaves used in cookery and for triumphal crowns; a brown horse with black points; a broad inlet of the sea; and a loud noise made by a dog?

Three bonus questions on cooking vegetables

a. Derived from a proper name, what term is used for vegetables when cut into small, thin strips?

b. What eight-letter word denotes a vegetable that has been cut into very small cubes?

c. What term denotes mixed vegetables cut into small pieces, and is derived from the name of an ancient empire that shares its name with a country in the Balkans?

The Answers

1 Cantonese
    a. *Timon of Athens*
    b. *Pale Fire* ('The Moon's an arrant thief / And her pale fire she snatches from the Sun')
    c. Wyndham Lewis

2 Etruria
    a. Florence
    b. Santa Croce
    c. Dante

3 Innit
    a. Gambit
    b. J'adoube (meaning 'I adjust')
    c. Rook (accept castle; 'minor pieces' are bishops and knights)

4 (Immanuel) Kant
    a. Ptolemy
    b. (Tycho) Brahe
    c. Galileo

5 Book tokens
    a. Henry the Sixth
    b. Haiti
    c. The Hundred Days

6 Cell and cello

   a. Flue and flute
   b. Moral and mortal
   c. Neuron and neutron

7 (Ebenezer) Scrooge (in *A Christmas Carol* by Charles Dickens, of course)
   a. Oysters
   b. *Death of a Salesman*
   c. Jonathan Swift

8 Granite (ingrate, Tangier, tearing)
   a. Purple
   b. Mouse
   c. (Bricks in) a wall

9 (Identity and) Passport Service
   a. (Sea of) Azov
   b. Azincourt
   c. Azores

10 (Karl Friedrich) Mohr (Mohr's Balance and Mohr's Salt)
   a. Nitrogen
   b. N-acetyl muramic acid (accept murnac; $C_{11}H_{19}NO_8$)
   c. Chitin

11 Vestibule
   a. Chimpanzee (if they answer 'primate' that is the order, not the species)
   b. Jane Goodall
   c. Cheeta

12 Russia
   a. War(s) of the Three Kingdoms
   b. Seven Years' War
   c. War of Jenkins' Ear

13 Belgium
- **a.** Martinique
- **b.** Strombolian eruptions (accept Stromboli, correcting it)
- **c.** Pliny the Elder / Gaius Plinius Secundus

14 Lumen
- **a.** Grasses (or true grasses)
- **b.** Rhizomes
- **c.** Rye

15 Liberia
- **a.** Iranian; Peace (2003)
- **b.** Austrian; Literature (2004)
- **c.** Israeli; Chemistry (2009)

16 (Marcus Tullius) Cicero
- **a.** Zephyr
- **b.** Hyacinth
- **c.** Solar-powered / by the Sun / solar cells (lithium sulphur batteries charged by sunlight)

17 Golden Raspberry Awards / Razzies
- **a.** (Thomas) Jefferson
- **b.** *Animal Farm*
- **c.** (Mark) Twain

18 (Alexander Graham) Bell
- **a.** Cotton
- **b.** Cotton gin
- **c.** Mercerising / mercerisation

19 125 metres
- **a.** Two (i.e. the identity and one rotation)
- **b.** Six (i.e. the identity, two rotations and three reflections)
- **c.** Sixteen (i.e. the identity, seven rotations and eight reflections)

20 Arabic (allow Islamic, Persian)
- **a.** Pidgin
- **b.** Creole
- **c.** Papua New Guinea

21 Little Ice Age
- **a.** The Wash
- **b.** Cader Idris
- **c.** Staffa

22 Creationism
- **a.** Cairo (al-Qahirah)
- **b.** *Bismarck*
- **c.** Idi Amin

23 Edinburgh
- **a.** Beijing
- **b.** Astana
- **c.** Ottawa

24 Hergé
- **a.** Oscar Wilde ('The Ballad of Reading Gaol')
- **b.** Emily Brontë
- **c.** Hamlet

25 Joan of Arc
- **a.** Winchester
- **b.** Lisieux
- **c.** Pilgrimage of Grace

26 Inception
- **a.** Luxembourg (2,586 sq km)
- **b.** Montenegro (13,800 sq km)
- **c.** United Kingdom (accept England)

27 Marianne (an anagram of Armenian, of course)

a. Angered (there are only three other single-word anagrams, none of which define the given word: grenade, derange, grandee)

b. Curtailment

c. Athletics

28 F.D. / Fidei Defensor / Defender of the Faith

a. Henry the Fourth (Henry of Navarre, Henry or Heinrich IV, Henry Bolingbroke)

b. Frederick the Second

c. George the First (of Greece, and of Great Britain)

29 Kurdish / Kurdic

a. (Fyodor) Dostoevsky

b. (Ivan) Turgenev

c. (Aleksandr) Solzhenitsyn

30 Bay

a. Julienne

b. Brunoise

c. Macedoine (from Macedonia, of course)

Match Thirteen

1 Which capital city is home to the Albertina, the Liechtenstein museum, and the former imperial residence the Schönbrunn Palace?

Three bonus questions on the Arab world

a. Also that of a city in Saudi Arabia, what name is given to the ancient quarter in various North African cities, and derives from the Arabic for 'town'?

b. From the Arabic for 'citadel', what word is used specifically for an area of the city of Algiers, and more generally for an old and often walled section of a city?

c. What short Arabic term denotes an open-air market-place or bazaar, for example al-Hamidiyeh in Damascus?

2 Standing at the end of the Royal Mile against the backdrop of Arthur's Seat, which Edinburgh palace is the official residence of the Queen in Scotland?

Three bonus questions on high stones

a. Lying about five miles north west of the moorland slopes of the Long Mynd, the Stiperstones are a ragged ridge of high hills in which English county?

b. Carn Menyn, the jagged rocky outcrops thought to have been the source of the bluestones used in Stonehenge, forms a part of which hills in West Wales?

c. The ruin of an observatory built in 1883 and a war memorial to the dead of the Second World War are among the manmade objects occupying the large stone plateau at the peak of which British mountain?

3 According to the US psychologist Robert J. Sternberg, what human mood or emotion can be described using the 'triangular theory', in which it is deconstructed into the three components of passion, intimacy and commitment?

Three bonus questions on nineteenth-century politics

a. After the Prime Minister who initially led them, what name was given to those Conservatives who remained committed to free trade after the repeal of the Corn Laws in 1846?

b. From a cave in which David gathered discontented followers in the Old Testament, 'Adullamites' was a derisive name given to those Liberals who brought about the fall of their government in 1866 on which issue?

c. The Liberal Unionists were a parliamentary group that emerged after a split over which issue in 1886?

4 Mark Twain wrote that 'A young lady has no sex, while a turnip has. Think what overwrought reverence that shows for the turnip, and what callous disrespect for the girl.' Which language was he describing, on account of the difficulty he had in learning it?

Three bonus questions on abbreviations

a. What two-letter abbreviation can signify both an imperial weight and, in cricket, a run made after the ball has touched any part of the batsman except his hands or the bat?

b. For what two-word phrase does the abbreviation LBO stand when it refers to the purchase of a company that is financed by borrowed capital?

c. LBA is the code for which UK international airport? It began operations as Yeadon Aerodrome in 1931.

5 What was the name of the twelfth-century claimant to the throne of England who was the daughter of Henry the First, the wife of the Holy Roman Emperor Henry the Fifth, and the mother of Henry the Second? Her cousin Stephen usurped the throne, and a civil war ensued.

Three bonus questions on the history of Afghanistan. In each case, I want the decade in which the following began.

a. The first Anglo-Afghan war, in which a British force failed to install a puppet ruler in Kabul and was destroyed during its retreat to the Khyber pass?

b. The third Anglo-Afghan war, in which an Afghan attack on British India achieved the formal recognition of Afghanistan's sovereignty at international law?

c. The Soviet war in Afghanistan, which supported the government of Afghanistan at its own request?

6 *Civil Disobedience* is a work of 1849 by which US author, also noted for *A Week on the Concord and Merrimack River* and *Walden*?

Three bonus questions on adjectives that end in the letters '-tory'. In each case, give the single word from the definition.

a. Imperious, dogmatic, admitting no denial, refusal, appeal or challenge?

b. Rambling, aimless, skipping from one thing to another in a half-hearted, unmethodical way?

c. Done merely as a token, for form's sake, hence superficial or careless?

7 In which order of mammals are the structures known as baleen plates seen? Composed of keratin, the plates are attached to the upper jaw and used for filter feeding.

Three bonus questions on mammalian physiology

a. The adenohypophysis is part of which gland, dominant in the regulation of the endocrine system?

b. Which gonadotrophic hormone produced by the adenohypophysis stimulates Leydig cells in males to produce testosterone?

c. From the Greek for 'extremities' and 'large', which medical condition is caused by excessive release of growth hormone in later life?

8 Listen carefully. The SI unit of time, the second, is defined in reference to the transition between two hyperfine levels of the ground state of a particular atom. What element is currently stipulated in this definition?

Three bonus questions on acids

a. Which fatty acid, soluble in alcohol and ether but practically insoluble in water, is used to make soap and candles; its name is derived from the Greek for 'fat' or 'tallow'?

b. Which white, crystalline carboxylic acid was first derived from rowan berries, and is used to inhibit mould growth?

c. Which poisonous acid used in the leather and ink industries is found in rhubarb leaves, and takes its name from the scientific name for wood sorrel, in which it occurs as a salt?

9 The tesseract, or four-dimensional hypercube, possesses how many corners?

Three bonus questions on cartography

a. Based on Gall's projection, which German historian published a controversial world map in 1973, described by one source as resembling 'winter underwear hung out to dry on the Arctic Circle', and representing the exact area of all countries in an accurate ratio?

b. Formerly described as zenithal, what term is now used for a map projection in which a region of the Earth is projected onto a plane tangential to the surface, usually at a pole or the Equator?

c. Introduced as a navigation tool in 1569, the Mercator map is an example of which form of projection?

10 What flower links a 1985 film directed by Woody Allen, a song by Edith Piaf, and novels by Iris Murdoch and Umberto Eco?

Three bonus questions on bacteria

a. From the Greek for 'to eat', what name is given to a virus that infects bacteria?

b. What name is given to the cycle in which phages incorporate their nucleic acid into the chromosome of the host cell and replicate with it as a unit without destroying the cell?

c. A lysogenic strain of the *streptococcus pyogenes* bacteria produces an erythrogenic toxin that leads to which illness, similar to strep throat, but with a characteristic red rash?

11 From the Russian for 'fist', what term indicates the higher-income farmers who emerged after the emancipation of the serfs in the nineteenth century, and who were then destroyed as a class by Stalin during his forced collectivisation of agriculture?

Three bonus questions on religious clothing

a. Usually made of wool, the *tallit* is a prayer shawl associated with which religion?

b. Consisting, for men, of two lengths of white cotton, *ihram* clothing is worn by those performing which of the five Pillars of Islam?

c. Part of the distinctive dress known as the *bana*, the term *dastaar* denotes what religious headwear?

12 Founded around 300 BC by Zeno of Citium, which school of philosophy is named after the colonnade in Athens in which its founder used to lecture?

Three bonus questions on silver anniversaries of 2011

a. 2011 marked the twenty-fifth anniversary of the Treaty of Canterbury, authorising which project? Proposed since the early nineteenth century, it had been feared by some to lead to the defacing of the countryside and the interruption of 'English habits of living'?

b. 2011 marked the twenty-fifth anniversary of the enthronement of which cleric and Nobel Prize winner as the first black South African Anglican Archbishop of Cape Town?

c. 2011 also marked twenty-five years of which film production company? Developing out of a division of Lucasfilm originally established in 1979, its output includes the 2008 film *WALL-E*, described by one critic as 'the *Citizen Kane* of animated films'?

13 In mathematics, the term 'sphere' refers strictly to a spherical surface. What short term is used for a solid sphere?

Three bonus questions on physics

a. Sometimes abbreviated to QCD, which branch of physics explains permissible combinations of quarks to form various elementary particles by the notional assignment of a primary colour to each?

b. In quantum chromodynamics, any one of the three complementary colours of cyan, magenta and yellow may be assigned to what?

c. When a quark combines with an anti-quark to form a meson, what is the resulting colour?

14 Answer as soon as you buzz. Name two of the three largest moons in the Solar System.

Three bonus questions on words meaning 'very big'

a. What word meaning 'very big' derives from a Greek term for a large statue and was applied by Herodotus to those of the temples of Egypt, although it later became associated with one particular figure in the Eastern Mediterranean?

b. The Greek name for the sons of Gaia who declared war on the gods and were destroyed by Heracles is the source of two common synonyms for 'enormous'. Name either of them.

c. Before the giants, Gaia had begotten a race of gods with Uranus, including Cronos and Rhea, whose collective name is the source of which adjective meaning 'very big'?

15 Popularised by the Hungarian Marxist Georg Lukacs as a means of generalising Marx's theory of commodity fetishism, what term refers to the process by which abstract concepts are treated as if they are tangible material objects? It derives from the Latin for 'thing'.

Three bonus questions on ancient Greece. In each case name the person described. To make it a little easier, all three have names that begin with the letters 'Ly-'.

a. An Athenian statesman born around 390; a supporter of Demosthenes, he was noted both for sound financial administration and for his public architectural works?

b. An orator born around 540 BC and noted for his clarity of thought and expression, for example in his speech against the Athenian tyrant Eratosthenes?

c. The Spartan commander who defeated Athens at the battle of Aegospotami in 405 BC and captured Athens the following year?

16 What surname links: an Australian poet born in 1833 and honoured in Westminster Abbey; the nineteenth-century Prime Minister Lord Aberdeen; and one of Lytton Strachey's *Eminent Victorians*, who died in 1885 at the end of the siege of Khartoum?

Three bonus questions on American universities

a. In American universities, first year students are generally called 'freshmen' and second years 'sophomores'. What term is used for third years?

b. The process known as graduation in British universities is known by what common term in American universities?

c. The distinguished academic society or fraternity 'Phi Beta Kappa' gets its name from the initial letters of the Greek motto 'Philosophia biou kybernetes'. What does this mean in English?

17 In which city is the velodrome that is Britain's first indoor Olympic cycling track and houses the National Cycling Centre?

Three bonus questions on place names, specifically, those that differ only in their final letter of the English spelling of their names, for example 'Peru' and 'Perm', in Russia. In each case, give both names from the description.

a. A New England state, and the capital of the German state of Rheinland-Pfalz?

b. A metropolitan borough of Merseyside, and an island in the South Atlantic with its capital at Jamestown?

c. An Italian river, and the region sometimes known as 'the Roof of the World'?

18 Listen carefully. Two groups have had three successive Christmas number one hit singles, the former in the 1960s, the latter in the 1990s. For ten points, name both.

Three bonus questions on merchants

a. 'The Merchant of Death Is Dead' was a headline of 1888 that erroneously announced the death of which Swedish inventor and industrialist, having confused him with his recently deceased brother?

b. *The Merchant of Yonkers* is a play of 1938 by which US writer, also known for the novel *The Bridge of San Luis Rey* and the play *Our Town*?

c. In Shakespeare's *The Merchant of Venice*, what is the name of the merchant taken to court by Shylock for his 'pound of flesh'?

19 Which century links: the beginning of the Gupta dynasty in India, the fall of the Han dynasty in China, the establishment of the Sassanid empire in Persia and the accession of the reforming Roman Emperor Diocletian?

Three bonus questions on modern political philosophers

a. A proponent of analytical Marxism who died in 2009, which political philosopher's works include *If You're an Egalitarian, How Come You're So Rich?*?

b. Born in 1939 in Mandate Palestine and a leading proponent of legal positivism, which philosopher's works include *The Authority of Law* and *The Morality of Freedom*?

c. Widely credited with the reinvigoration of modern political philosophy, which US philosopher is noted for the dictum that the principles of justice must be chosen behind a 'veil of ignorance'?

20 Answer as soon as you buzz. Since 1961, four US state governors have gone on to become President, the most recent being George W. Bush. For ten points, name two of the others.

Three bonus questions on a shared name

a. Which US President was re-elected in November 1916 under the campaign slogan 'He kept us out of the war'?

b. Woodrow Wilson were the first two given names of which American folk singer, best known for his 'Dust Bowl Ballads' and the song 'This Land Is Your Land'?

c. The American astronomer Robert Woodrow Wilson is jointly credited, with the German-born Arno Allan Penzias, with the discovery in 1964 of C.M.B.; for what do these initials stand?

21 Answer as soon as you buzz. Give the dictionary spelling of the first half of the binomial 'e.coli', that is, 'escherichia'?

Three bonus questions on a shared term

a. What adjective, meaning 'of mixed character', derives from a Latin term denoting offspring such as that of a freeman and a slave, or a tame sow and a wild boar?

b. The name of which hybrid animal may also denote hybrid machines such as the one developed by Samuel Crompton in 1779 that combined a Spinning Jenny with Arkwright's Water Frame?

c. Which mythological hybrid is the offspring of a griffin and a mare, and appears in Canto Four of the sixteenth-century poem 'Orlando Furioso'?

22 Sterling silver is an alloy of 92.5 per cent silver with, most commonly, which other element that serves to harden the metal?

Three bonus questions on medical abbreviations

a. A non-invasive procedure used to visualise internal structures in various examinations, for what do the letters MRI stand?

b. A CT scan employs digital processing of X-ray images to produce a three-dimensional image of internal structures. For what do the letters CT stand?

c. What three-letter abbreviation denotes the non-invasive recording of the electrical activity of the heart over time, using electrodes placed at various locations on the skin?

23 Answer as soon as you buzz. Which is the only vowel that does not appear on the topmost row of letters in the standard layout of a UK English language keyboard?

Three bonus questions on English words from Asian languages

a. From Japanese characters meaning 'great lord', what term was formerly used as a title of the Shogun, but now describes a business or industrial magnate?

b. From the Mandarin for 'work together', what phrase means excessively or unthinkingly eager, especially in the context of patriotism and military aggression?

c. The word 'paddy', meaning 'rice field', derives from the word for 'rice plant' in which major Southeast Asian language?

24 What specific human disposition is both 'provoked' and 'unprovoked' by drink, according to the Porter in Shakespeare's *Macbeth*?

Three bonus questions on writers' opinions of Shakespeare

a. Born in 1885, which poet and novelist's poem 'When I Read Shakespeare' includes these lines? 'And Hamlet, how boring, how boring to live with, / So mean and self-conscious, blowing and snoring / His wonderful speeches, full of other folk's whoring!'

b. In his 1668 essay 'Of Dramatic Poesy', who described Shakespeare as 'many times flat, insipid; his comic wit degenerating into clenches, his serious swelling into bombast. But he is always great when some great occasion is presented to him'?

c. In a letter of March 1814, which poet wrote: 'Shakespeare's name, you may depend upon it, stands absurdly too high; he took all his plots from old novels, and threw their stories into a dramatic shape'?

25 What fraction links: mercy to someone who has surrendered; an area of a city; a phase of the Moon; 25 cents; and, in the plural, lodgings for soldiers?

Three bonus questions on horses in classical poetry

a. 'The brave are born from the brave and good. In steers and in horses is to be found the excellence of their sire; nor do savage eagles produce a peaceful dove.' These are the words of which Roman poet in his *Odes*?

b. In his *Georgics*, which Roman poet wrote: 'And when the rising sun has first breathed on us with his panting horses, over there the red evening-star is lighting his late lamps'?

c. When Marlowe's Doctor Faustus faces the arrival of Lucifer to claim his soul and cries, 'O lente, lente currite, noctis equi' ('Run slowly, horses of the night'), he is quoting which Roman poet?

26 Two large islands are divided by international land frontiers that measure around 360 kilometres. One is Hispaniola, in the Caribbean; what is the other?

Three bonus questions on divided islands

a. The western half of the island of New Guinea and about two-thirds of the island of Borneo belong to which Asian country?

b. Which South American archipelago is separated from the mainland by the Strait of Magellan, and is divided between Chile and Argentina?

c. The island of Usedom or Uznam, on the Baltic Coast, is divided between which two countries?

27 *Bergamia, sinensis* and *aurantium* are three species of which citrus fruit? Their common names are Bergamot, Sweet and Seville?

Three bonus questions on expressions in which the last two letters of the first word and the first two letters of the second word are the same, for example 'apple lemonade' or 'tomato torte'. In each case, give the name of the food or drink from the definition.

a. A Japanese dish in which fermented bean paste is mixed with a stock called 'dashi'?

b. An infusion of *Camellia sinensis*, flavoured with *Theobroma cacao*?

c. Cheese from North Holland that has been cured, for example, over a wood fire?

28 Quote: 'I have spent much of my life fighting the Germans and fighting the politicians. It is much easier to fight the Germans.' These are the words of which military commander, in a speech marking the twenty-fifth anniversary of the Battle of el Alamein?

Three bonus questions on Europe and Asia

a. By convention one of the boundaries between Europe and Asia, which mountain range includes Mount Elbrus, generally considered to be the highest point in Europe?

b. Which major Russian river, known in Greek as 'Tánaïs', was in ancient times regarded as the boundary between Europe and Asia?

c. '... Nor have I been able to learn who it was that first marked these boundaries, or where they got the names from.' Which ancient Greek author made this observation in his *Histories*?

29 What single word is the motto of the state of California? One of the few state mottos not in English or Latin, it means 'I have found it' and is associated with Archimedes.

Three bonus questions on black and white flags

a. Consisting of nine black and white horizontal stripes with the top-left quarter spotted to symbolise ermine, the Gwenn-ha-du flag is the official flag of which region of France?

b. A moor's head in black with a white bandana on a white background comprises the flag of which Mediterranean island?

c. Established in 1701 and part of Germany from 1871, which kingdom had a variety of black and white flags, ultimately derived from the banner of the Teutonic knights?

30 Listen carefully and answer as soon as you buzz. What is 'a', if 'g' is 289, 'f' is 169 and 'e' is 121?

Three bonus questions on exotic materials

a. What term refers to artificially engineered materials with optical or electromagnetic properties not found in nature?

b. Referring to a twentieth-century Soviet scientist, what two-word term indicates the blue glow associated with nuclear reactors, caused by a charged particle moving through a di-electric medium faster than the local speed of light?

c. Occurring when Cherenkov radiation is emitted behind the particle travelling through the medium, the reverse Cherenkov effect has been observed in meta-materials with what optical property?

The Answers

1 Vienna
    a.   Medina (not Kasbah)
    b.   Casbah / kasbah
    c.   Souk / suq

2 (Palace of) Holyroodhouse
    a.   Shropshire
    b.   Preseli Hills
    c.   Ben Nevis

3 Love
    a.   Peelite
    b.   Parliamentary reform / franchise reform (accept similar)
    c.   Irish home rule

4 German ('The Awful German Language')
    a.   Lb (weight – Latin: *libra*; cricket – leg bye)
    b.   Leveraged Buyout
    c.   Leeds Bradford (International Airport)

5 (Empress) Matilda (accept Maude)
    a.   1830s (1838–1842)
    b.   1910s (1919)
    c.   1970s (December 1979)

6 (Henry David) Thoreau
    a.   Peremptory
    b.   Desultory

c.   Perfunctory (accept nugatory)

⑦ *Cetacea* / whales
    a.   Pituitary gland / pituitary body / hypophysis
    b.   Luteinizing hormone (accept L.H.)
    c.   Acromegaly

⑧ Caesium (133)
    a.   Stearic (acid)
    b.   Sorbic (acid)
    c.   Oxalic (acid)

⑨ Sixteen
    a.   (Arno) Peters
    b.   Azimuthal
    c.   Cylindrical

⑩ Rose (*Purple Rose of Cairo*, 'La Vie en Rose', *An Unofficial Rose*, *Name of the Rose*)
    a.   Phage (accept bacteriophage)
    b.   Lysogenic (cycle) or lysogeny
    c.   Scarlet fever or Scarlatina

⑪ Kulaks / kulaki
    a.   Judaism
    b.   Hajj / pilgrimage to Mecca
    c.   (Sikh) Turban

⑫ Stoicism (the Stoa Poikile, or 'painted porch')
    a.   The Channel Tunnel
    b.   (Most Reverend Dr) Desmond Tutu
    c.   Pixar (Animation Studios)

⑬ Ball (accept disk; physicists do not use the term 'ball' but mathematicians do)
    a.   Quantum chromodynamics

    b.   Anti-quarks

    c.   White

14 Ganymede, Titan, Callisto
    a.   Colossal / colossus
    b.   Gigantic / giant
    c.   Titanic

15 Reification
    a.   Lycurgus (there was also a mythical Spartan lawgiver called Lycurgus)
    b.   Lysias
    c.   Lysander

16 Gordon (Adam Lindsay, 1833–1870; George Hamilton, 1784–1860; General Charles, 1833–1885)
    a.   Juniors (fourth years are 'seniors')
    b.   Commencement
    c.   Philosophy (is) the guide of life (or Love of learning is the guide to life)

17 Manchester
    a.   Maine and Mainz
    b.   St Helens and St Helena
    c.   Tiber and Tibet

18 The Beatles and The Spice Girls
    a.   Alfred Nobel
    b.   Thornton Wilder
    c.   Antonio

19 Third (201–300; 240, 220, 224, 284)
    a.   Gerald Cohen
    b.   (Joseph) Raz
    c.   John Rawls

20 Carter / Reagan / Clinton (Georgia 1971–1975; California 1967–1975; Arkansas 1979–1981, 1983–1992)
- **a.** (Thomas) Woodrow Wilson
- **b.** Woody Guthrie
- **c.** Cosmic Microwave Background (radiation)

21 E.s.c.h.e.r.i.c.h.i.a.
- **a.** Hybrid
- **b.** Mule
- **c.** Hippogryph

22 Copper
- **a.** Magnetic Resonance Imaging
- **b.** Computer Tomography (accept Computed Tomography)
- **c.** ECG / EKG

23 'A' (which appears on the second row of letters)
- **a.** Tycoon
- **b.** Gung-ho (from 'gonghe')
- **c.** Malay / Bahasa Indonesia

24 Lechery ('Lechery, sir ... It provokes the desire, but it takes away the performance.')
- **a.** D.H. Lawrence
- **b.** John Dryden
- **c.** Lord Byron

25 Quarter
- **a.** Horace
- **b.** Virgil
- **c.** Ovid

26 Ireland (New Guinea is only 820 km; Timor is 228 km)
- **a.** Indonesia
- **b.** Tierra del Fuego
- **c.** Germany and Poland

27 Orange
- **a.** Miso soup
- **b.** Chocolate tea
- **c.** Smoked Edam

28 (Lord) Montgomery
- **a.** Caucasus
- **b.** Don
- **c.** Herodotus

29 Eureka
- **a.** Brittany
- **b.** Corsica
- **c.** Prussia

30 4 (squares of primes in descending order, so 'd' is 49, 'c' is 25, etc.
- **a.** Meta-materials
- **b.** Cherenkov radiation (or light or glow)
- **c.** Negative refractive index

Match Fourteen

1 The Golestan Palace and the Azadi Tower are among prominent buildings in which capital city, located around 100 kilometres south of the Caspian Sea?

Three bonus questions on Dante's *Inferno*

    a. In Dante's *Inferno*, how many concentric circles of suffering lie within the Earth?

    b. In the second circle of Hell, those guilty of which sin are punished by being blown about by the winds of a violent storm? It is here that Dante meets Helen of Troy, Dido and Cleopatra.

    c. In the eighth circle, those guilty of which vice are condemned to wear golden cloaks weighted down with lead?

2 In coastal geography, what two-word term denotes the zig-zag movement of material, such as pebbles, along a beach? Caused by waves striking at an angle, over time it erodes the beach and forms ridges of sand or shingle which project into the sea.

Three bonus questions on Florentine architecture

    a. Dedicated to Saint John, which building in Florence has a gilded bronze door known as 'the Gates of Paradise', designed by Lorenzo Ghiberti?

b. Which of Ghiberti's contemporaries was the architect who designed the Basilica of San Lorenzo, begun in 1418, and gave a practical demonstration of the geometric method of perspective?

c. Which square or piazza lies in front of the Palazzo Vecchio, its features including Cellini's statue of Perseus with the head of Medusa?

3 Walking down a street throwing litter, winding a clock in a songwriter's apartment, standing on a street in a cowboy hat, and walking two dogs out of a pet shop; from 1935 onwards, these were among the cameo appearances of which director in his own films?

Three bonus questions on words that can be made from the seven letters of the word 'lyrical'. In each case, give the word from the description.

a. A small tree of the genus *Syringa*, whose fragrant blossom gives its name to a pale, pinkish-violet colour?

b. A covering or appendage of some seeds, for example, the red fleshy cup around the seed of a yew tree?

c. A portion of a curve, or a luminous discharge between two electrodes?

4 Meaning 'whey' or 'watery fluid', what term denotes the greenish-yellow liquid that separates from the clot when blood coagulates? When taken from an animal that has been inoculated with bacteria or their toxins, it is used for immunisation.

Three bonus questions on paintings in the National Gallery. In each case, name the British monarch who was on the throne when the following were painted.

a. *Mr and Mrs Andrews* by Thomas Gainsborough?

b. *The Hay Wain* by John Constable?

c. *The Fighting Temeraire* by Turner?

5 What symbolic figure was addressed by Madame Roland, the wife of the French minister of the interior, before her execution in the Place de la Révolution in 1793 when she said, 'What crimes are committed in thy name'?

Three bonus questions on a judicial issue

a. Which decade saw the establishment of the guidelines known as 'Judges' Rules', which enshrined the right of a suspect in a criminal case to remain silent under questioning without prejudice at a subsequent trial?

b. Amending the right to silence by allowing a jury to draw adverse inferences from a defendant's reliance in court on something not mentioned in questioning, the bill that became the 1994 Criminal Justice and Public Order Act was introduced by which Home Secretary?

c. Coined in 1966, what name is given to the rights, including the right to remain silent, of a criminal suspect in the USA?

6 In ancient Greece, a Myriarch was a commander of how many men?

Three bonus questions on codes

a. Its statutes including the Conventicle Act and the Five-Mile Act, a 'code' aimed at restricting the activity of nonconformists in seventeenth-century England is often named after which Lord Chancellor?

b. Which Chinese dynasty gives its name to a penal code of 624 CE that became the basis for later dynastic codes in China and other East Asian states?

c. Effective in the USA from the 1930s to the 1960s, the Hays Code regulated what form of artistic expression?

7 The Australian philosopher D.C. Stove used the name of which fictional character to describe an 'effect' whereby a philosophical theory makes a sole exception of itself, and thereby claims to escape from the fate to which it condemns all other discourse? The idea comes from the words 'And I only am escaped alone to tell thee' in the character's epilogue to *Moby-Dick*.

Three bonus questions on literature. In each case, give the title of the early twentieth-century novel the opening lines of which mention the following locations.

a. 'The Marsh Farm, in the meadows where the Erewash twisted sluggishly through alder trees, separating Derbyshire from Nottinghamshire'?

b. '"The cave" ... a large old-fashioned three-storied building ... about a mile outside the town of Mugsborough'?

c. 'The Marabar caves... [twenty miles from] the city of Chandrapore'?

8 Named after a Pacific atoll that had been the site of nuclear testing a few days earlier, which garment was first modelled by Micheline Bernardini of Paris in July 1946?

Three bonus questions on place names

a. Its name believed to derive from a Celtic term for 'cave', which limestone cavern in the Mendip Hills in Somerset has yielded finds of prehistoric implements and contains a stalagmite which, according to legend, was formerly a witch?

   b. The Hole of Horcum, which, according to local legend, was scooped out of the landscape by a giant, lies south of the village of Goathland in which English national park?

   c. Hole, or Heu-lah, formed part of the historical region of Ringerike in Norway and was the home of which eleventh-century king, who was killed when he invaded England in 1066?

9 During a concert at Manchester's Free Trade Hall on 17 May 1966, what name, shouted by an audience member, elicited the response 'I don't believe you. You're a liar' from Bob Dylan?

Three bonus questions on beds

   a. Which three-metre-wide bed dominates Room 57 of the Victoria and Albert Museum, and was probably built for an inn in Hertfordshire in about 1590?

   b. Consisting of a pillow, sheet and quilt supported on a frame, the 1955 work *Bed* was among which US artist's first 'Combines', the term he used for artworks incorporating cast-off items such as old material or furniture?

   c. Which Turner Prize-nominated artist exhibited the installation *My Bed* at the Tate Britain in 1999?

10 In an essay of 1953, the philosopher Isaiah Berlin drew on the writings attributed to the Greek poet Archilochus and used which two animals to illustrate the tension between monist and pluralist visions of history, by stating that there are people who know many things, while others know one big thing?

Three bonus questions on a shared surname

a. Observable as the effect of a strong electric field on radiating atoms, ions or molecules, the splitting of spectral lines is named after which German physicist, who first described it in 1913?

b. 1932 saw the publication of the first work by the British travel writer Dame Freya Stark, and consisted of her sketches of which Middle Eastern city?

c. Born in 1794, the landscape painter James Stark was a member of the artistic school associated with which English cathedral city?

11 In 1824, the Norwegian mathematician Niels Henrik Abel proved that there is no general formula involving radicals for the solution of polynomial equations of which degree?

Three bonus questions on a ritual

a. Meaning 'act of faith', what three-word phrase is used for the burning at the stake of heretics condemned by the inquisition, last carried out in Spain in 1781 and in Mexico in 1815?

b. 'The burning of a few people alive by a slow fire, and with great ceremony, is an infallible preventative of earthquakes' wrote Voltaire, attacking the rituals carried out after the devastation by earthquake in 1755 of which European city?

c. An Auto da Fe begins at the end of the third act of which opera by Verdi, based on a play by Schiller, its title character being a sixteenth-century prince of Asturias?

12 In physics, what polysyllabic word describes the emission of light from a fluid caused by the passage of sound waves through it?

Three bonus questions on physics

a. What physical quantity is equivalent to momentum flux or stress, expressed in SI base units as kilogrammes per metre per second squared?

b. What manometric unit of pressure is equal to 1.33 millibars?

c. If the weather is such that standard atmospheric pressure obtains at sea level, at what integer number of kilometres altitude would you experience a pressure of about 600 torr?

13 In embryology, what structure is formed by invagination of the blastula, which then forms the primitive gut known as the archenteron?

Three bonus questions on twentieth-century history

a. The Sykes-Picot Agreement of 1916 between Britain and France dealt with the partition of which empire after the end of the First World War?

b. The Hoare-Laval Pact of 1935, later repudiated by Britain because of the outcry it created, effectively legitimised which act of aggression?

c. Which two foreign ministers gave their names to the pact of 1939 that agreed, amongst other things, to the partitioning of Poland?

14 Born in 1878, which French chemist gives his name to a reaction between protein and carbohydrate that results in non-enzymic browning, for example in toasting bread?

Three bonus questions on chemistry

a. What term describes a compound such as aluminium hydroxide that can act as both an acid and a base?

b. When aluminium hydroxide reacts with an acid it produces an aluminium salt. What is the product when it reacts with a base?

c. Which weak dibasic acid is produced when carbon dioxide dissolves in water?

15 Answer as soon as you buzz. Which words would appear first and last if the colours of the rainbow were written in alphabetical order?

Three bonus questions on an artist

a. The nineteenth-century Dutch landscape painter Anton Mauve was married to the cousin of which fellow artist, to whom he gave help and instruction early in his career?

b. Now in the Pushkin Museum of Fine Art in Moscow, which painting by Van Gogh sold for 400 francs a few months before his death, and is popularly believed to be the only painting he sold during his lifetime?

c. In 1888, to which town in Provence did Van Gogh escape from his life in Paris, in order to set up his so-called 'studio of the south'?

16 Appearing on the edge of a commemorative £5 coin, the inscription 'Be daring, be first, be different, be just' is attributed to which businesswoman, human rights activist and environmental campaigner, who died in 2007?

Three bonus questions on British coins

a. Since September 1992, which two British coins have been made of copper-plated steel?

b. The alloy used for five, ten, twenty and fifty pence coins consists principally of which two metallic elements?

c. The two pound coin has a cupronickel centre and an outer ring made of which alloy, also used to make one pound coins?

17 Also known as *The World Well Lost*, which tragedy by John Dryden portrays the last few hours of the lives of Antony and Cleopatra? In its day it was a more popular version of the story than the play by Shakespeare.

Three bonus questions on literature

a. Newland Archer, a young man in nineteenth-century New York society, is the protagonist of which novel of 1920 by Edith Wharton?

b. William Blake's *Songs of Innocence* were first published in 1789 and then republished in 1794 in a combined volume with which other collection?

c. In which novel of 1954 does the protagonist weep, quote, 'for the end of innocence, the darkness of man's heart, and the fall through the air of the true, wise friend called Piggy'?

18 Which is the only group of the periodic table to include elements existing in the form of all three states of matter at standard pressure and temperature?

Three bonus questions on an element

a. On what would have been his 537th birthday, the International Union of Pure and Applied Chemistry confirmed on 19 February 2010 that element number 112 had been named after which scientist?

b. As element number 112, copernicium was made by fusing isotopes of which two familiar metallic elements with atomic numbers 30 and 82?

    c.   Copernicium was discovered at the Helmholtz centre in Darmstadt in Germany, which had also isolated the previous five new elements, numbers 107 to 111. Five points if you can name two of them.

19 The dominant terrestrial tetrapod vertebrates prior to the dinosaurs, animals belonging to which class of amniotes, living from around 300 million years ago, are regarded as the ancestors of true mammals?

> **Three bonus questions on words that can be made from the seven letters of the word 'oarsman'. In each case, give word from the description.**
>
> **a.**   A gigantic, extinct New Zealand bird, resembling an ostrich?
>
> **b.**   The plural of the term for the third stomach of a ruminant?
>
> **c.**   An acronym for the paperwork needed for a registered vehicle that is not being used on the public highway?

20 Listen carefully. The Irish province of Connacht comprises five counties. Two are Leitrim and Roscommon. For ten points, name two of the others.

> **Three bonus questions on geography. In each case, give the next country whose territory you reach if you head due west from the following capital cities. For example, 'Lisbon' would give the answer 'USA'.**
>
> **a.**   Kiev?
>
> **b.**   Bangkok?
>
> **c.**   Cairo?

21 Give any of the three near-homophones that mean 'incense burner', 'one who decides what is fit to publish' and 'device for detecting movement'?

Three bonus questions on a craft

a. In what traditional craft might one find oneself following a four-word instruction represented by the abbreviation 'ktbl'?

b. For what does the letter 'y' stand in the knitting pattern instruction: 'yfon'?

c. Again in a knitting pattern, for what does 'sl1, k1, psso' stand?

22 In 1488 and 1513, two successive kings of Scotland died in battle. For ten points, name both.

Three bonus questions on history. In each case, I want the century which began with the following on the thrones of their respective countries.

a. Sweyn Forkbeard of Denmark, Otto the Third of the Holy Roman Empire, and Ethelred the Unready of England?

b. Ahuitzotl of the Aztecs, Ferdinand the Second of Aragon, and James the Fourth of Scotland?

c. Abdulhamid the Second of the Ottoman Empire, Leopold the Second of the Belgians, and Wilhelmina of the Netherlands?

23 In terms of population, what state is to the USA as Uttar Pradesh is to India, Sao Paulo to Brazil and New South Wales to Australia?

Three bonus questions on cities in the US state of Ohio

  a. Which city on Lake Erie by the border with Michigan shares its name with a historic city and world heritage site south of Madrid?

  b. Situated on the Ohio-Kentucky border, which city is named after a Roman dictator of the fifth century BC who returned to his farm after victory in battle, and was thus seen as embodying the ideal of selfless service to the Republic?

  c. Which city on Lake Erie close to the border with Pennsylvania is home to both the online comic-strip character Yehuda Moon and the Rock and Roll Hall of Fame?

24 Produced by Studio Ghibli in Japan, the animated film *Arrietty* is based on which children's novel by Mary Norton?

Three bonus questions on a Russian writer

  a. A poem based on a fairy tale and adapted as an opera by Rimsky-Korsakov, 'The Tale of Tsar Saltan' was written by which Russian literary figure, fatally injured in a duel in 1837?

  b. Which Russian Tsar, who ruled from 1598 to 1605, is the subject of a play by Pushkin and an opera by Mussorgsky?

  c. 'The Bronze Horseman' is a narrative poem by Pushkin about an equestrian statue of which Tsar? It stands in the city he founded on the banks of the Neva in 1703.

25 Founded in 1826 as a satirical weekly gossip sheet on the arts, which newspaper is now France's oldest daily paper, and is named after a character who appears in operas by Rossini and Mozart?

Three bonus questions on a letter of the alphabet

a. What letter, standing for the German for 'source', is used to symbolise the hypothetical document used by Matthew and Luke for many of the shared passages in their Gospels?

b. 'Q' was the pen-name of the poet and academic Arthur Quiller-Couch, noted for editing which work, which first appeared in 1900 and was revised by him in 1939?

c. In the Broadway musical *Avenue Q*, what question is posed by the character Princeton in the title of his song which includes the lines: 'Four years of college and plenty of knowledge / Have earned me this useless degree'?

26 Which six-letter word links a feature of adult earthworms known as the clitellum; a cut of meat containing the loin area; and a region of a geometrical surface that is a local minimum in one direction and a local maximum in another?

Three bonus questions on invasive species

a. What is the common name of *Lates niloticus*, whose introduction to Africa's Lake Victoria from the 1950s has led to the possible extinction of numerous endemic fish species?

b. Named after their hairy claws, which aggressive crabs, considered a delicacy in East Asia, have infested the Thames and other English rivers?

c. Introduced to control Australia's grayback beetle population, what is the common two-word name of the pest *Bufo marinus*?

27 Bean, Mitchell, Irwin, Cernan and Schmitt are the surnames of five of the twelve men who performed what specific feat between 1969 and 1972?

Three bonus questions on astronomy

a. Launched in February 2010 on a five-year mission to observe the Sun and its magnetic field, for what do the letters SDO stand?

b. What two-word term describes the massive explosions in the Sun's atmosphere as seen in the first-light images from the SDO?

c. Solar flare activity is associated with the presence of regions of intense magnetic activity but reduced temperature on the surface of the Sun. How are these regions known?

28 In geological time, what is the third and most recent epoch of the Palaeogene period, following the Eocene and preceding the Miocene?

Three bonus questions on geology

a. Which specific branch of geology is concerned with fossils and their use in dating rock layers?

b. Widely used in biostratigraphy, fossils that are useful for dating and correlating the strata in which they are found are known by what term?

c. Key indices for stratigraphical investigations, which fossils are the remains of a marine cephalopod mollusc from the Mesozoic era with a flat, tightly coiled shell?

29 Resulting from the action of sulphuric acid upon alcohol, which colourless, volatile liquid shares its name with the substance once believed to pervade all space, and thought necessary for the propagation of electromagnetic waves?

Three bonus questions on measuring instruments

a. From the Greek meaning 'drink measure', what name is given to an instrument which measures the water uptake of a leafy shoot?

b. A hydrometer measures the relative density of a liquid. What does a hygrometer measure?

c. From the Greek for 'path', what mechanical or electrical instrument measures distance travelled?

30 In physiology, what is stored in cells known as adipocytes?

Three bonus questions on a part of the body

a. *Plantar fasciitis* is a painful inflammation of a thick fibrous band of connective tissue in what part of the human body?

b. Other than bursitis, what name is commonly given to an inflamed swelling on the foot, especially of the bursa on the ball of the big toe?

c. Gout, which most commonly occurs in the toes, is caused by raised levels of which acid in the blood? It crystallises and is deposited in joints, tendons and surrounding tissues.

The Answers

1 Tehran
- **a.** Nine
- **b.** Lust
- **c.** Hypocrisy

2 Longshore drift
- **a.** The Baptistery
- **b.** (Filippo) Brunelleschi
- **c.** (Piazza) Della Signoria

3 Alfred Hitchcock (*The 39 Steps / Rear Window / Psycho / The Birds*)
- **a.** Lilac
- **b.** Aril
- **c.** Arc

4 (Blood) Serum
- **a.** George the Second
- **b.** George the Fourth
- **c.** Victoria

5 Liberty
- **a.** 1910s (1912)
- **b.** Michael Howard
- **c.** (The) Miranda Rights (US court ruling from the case Miranda v Arizona)

6 10,000
- **a.** (Earl of) Clarendon (Edward Hyde)

b. Tang

c. Film / cinema

(7) Ishmael (effect)

    a. *The Rainbow* (D.H. Lawrence, 1915; not the sequel, *Women in Love*, which opens differently)

    b. *The Ragged-Trousered Philanthropists* (Robert Tressell, 1914)

    c. *A Passage to India* (E.M. Forster, 1924)

(8) Bikini

    a. Wookey Hole

    b. North York Moors

    c. Harald Hardrada (accept Harald the Third [Sigurdsson])

(9) 'Judas'

    a. (The) Great Bed of Ware

    b. (Robert) Rauschenberg

    c. Tracey Emin

(10) Hedgehog and fox (fox knows many things; hedgehog knows one big thing)

    a. (Johannes) Stark

    b. Baghdad

    c. Norwich

(11) Fifth degree (accept five or quintic)

    a. Auto da Fe

    b. Lisbon

    c. *Don Carlos*

(12) Sonoluminescence

    a. Pressure

    b. Torr, or millimetre of mercury

    c. Two

⑬ Gastrula
- **a.** Ottoman (accept Turkish)
- **b.** Italian invasion of Abyssinia (or of Ethiopia; the second Italo-Abyssinian War)
- **c.** (Vyacheslav) Molotov and (Joachim von) Ribbentrop

⑭ (Louis Camille) Maillard (Maillard reaction)
- **a.** Amphoteric (accept amphiprotic)
- **b.** (An) Aluminate
- **c.** Carbonic (acid)

⑮ Blue and yellow
- **a.** Vincent van Gogh
- **b.** *The Red Vineyard / La Vigne Rouge*
- **c.** Arles

⑯ Anita Roddick (the coin marked the seventieth anniversary of Churchill becoming PM)
- **a.** One penny and two pence
- **b.** Copper and nickel (i.e. cupronickel)
- **c.** Nickel-brass

⑰ *All for Love*
- **a.** *The Age of Innocence*
- **b.** *Songs of Experience*
- **c.** *Lord of the Flies*

⑱ Halogen group / Group 17 (accept Group VIIB in the old IUPAC system; accept Group VIIA in the CAS system)
- **a.** (Nicolaus) Copernicus
- **b.** Zinc and lead
- **c.** Bohrium / hassium / meitnerium / darmstadtium / roentgenium

⑲ Synapsida / synapsids (not therapsid(a), which is a sub-group, also ancestral to mammals, but originated about 270 million years ago)

a. Moa
b. Omasa
c. SORN (Statutory Off-Road Notification)

20 Sligo, Galway, Mayo
a. Poland
b. Burma / Myanmar
c. Libya

21 Censer / censor / senser
a. Knitting (i.e. knit through back loop)
b. Yarn (i.e. yarn forward over needle)
c. Slip one (stitch) , knit one, pass slipped stitch over

22 James the Third and Fourth (the battles of Sauchieburn and Flodden respectively)
a. Eleventh century (c.986–1014, 996–1002 and 978–1016; Otto III was also German king 983–1002)
b. Sixteenth century (1486–1502, 1479–1516, 1488–1513)
c. Twentieth century (1876–1909, 1865–1909, 1890–1948)

23 California (most populous state in respective country, of course)
a. Toledo
b. Cincinnati (Lucius Quinctius Cincinnatus)
c. Cleveland

24 *The Borrowers*
a. (Alexander) Pushkin
b. Boris Godunov
c. Peter the Great / the First

25 *Le Figaro*
a. Q (for Quelle)
b. *The Oxford Book of English Verse (1250–1900)*

c.   'What can you do with a BA in English?'

26 Saddle

    a.   Nile perch

    b.   Mitten crabs (also known as big sluice crab, shanghai crab, hairy crab)

    c.   Cane toad

27 Walked on the Moon

    a.   Solar Dynamics Observatory

    b.   Solar flares

    c.   Sunspots

28 Oligocene (33.9 million to 23 million years ago)

    a.   Biostratigraphy

    b.   Index fossils (accept guide / indicator / zone fossils)

    c.   Ammonites

29 Ether

    a.   Potometer

    b.   Humidity (accept relative humidity / moisture content in the environmental air)

    c.   Odometer (not mileometer)

30 Fat / lipids / triacyl-glycerols / triglycerides

    a.   The foot (specifically the sole of the foot; the tissue runs from the heel to the toes and supports the arch of the foot)

    b.   Bunion

    c.   Uric acid

Match Fifteen

1 Listen carefully. In the two-dimensional plane, what is the scalar product of unit vector along the x-axis, and unit vector along the y-axis?

Three bonus questions on a British physicist

a. Which physicist constructed the first X-ray spectrometer in 1913, using it, with his son Lawrence, to determine crystal structures on the basis that X-rays passing through them are defracted by the regular array of atoms within the crystal?

b. Occurring close to the end of the path followed by particles, the Bragg Peak distinguishes the energy loss of which form of radiation during its movement through matter?

c. In an attributed remark, Bragg observed that 'physicists use the wave theory on Mondays, Wednesdays and Fridays,' and which other theory of light for the rest of the week?

2 'Quakes', 'fuse', 'skua' and 'ukase' are among words that may be made with letters of which adjective? Meaning 'impenetrably oppressive, senseless or disorienting', it is an eponym of a novelist born in Prague in 1883.

Three bonus questions on regencies

a. Richard, Duke of Gloucester, later Richard the Third, acted as regent during the minority of which king, his nephew, in 1483?

b. The Lord Chancellor and Bishop of Ely William Longchamp served as regent during the absence of which monarch on the third crusade?

c. Which of Henry the Eighth's wives ruled as his regent while he led a military expedition to France in the summer of 1544?

3 According to E.M. Forster, which French novelist altered his clock's hands 'so that his hero was at the same period entertaining his mistress to supper, and playing ball with his nurse in the park'?

Three bonus questions on seaside settings in fiction

a. In which novel of 2007 by Ian McEwan do Edward and Florence spend their wedding night at a hotel on the Dorset coast?

b. Dickens's David Copperfield describes which town on the Norfolk coast as 'rather spongy and soppy', only to be told that it 'was, upon the whole, the finest place in the universe'?

c. Set in a Sussex seaside town which the entrepreneurial Mr Parker hopes to develop into a fashionable resort, 'Sanditon' is an unfinished novel by which author?

4 Which vegetable links the dishes 'caponata', 'baba ghanoush' and 'imam bayildi'?

Three bonus questions on Irish counties. In each case, give the county name that corresponds to the surname of each of the following.

   a.   The presidential nominee of the Democratic Party in the 2004 US presidential election?

   b.   A poet from Northamptonshire, author of the 1820 *Poems Descriptive of Rural Life and Scenery*?

   c.   A detective who first appeared in the 1964 work *From Doon with Death* by Ruth Rendell?

5 In 2010, an unmanned spacecraft from which country became the first to return a sample of an asteroid to Earth, after a seven-year mission to a near-Earth object first discovered in 1998?

Three bonus questions on relative distances in astronomy

   a.   Imagine a circle of 1 centimetre diameter on a piece of paper. That's Earth. Now imagine another circle, 3 millimetres in diameter. That's the Moon. To the nearest 10 centimetres, how far will the 'Moon' circle be from the 'Earth' circle, using the same scale?

   b.   Using the same scale, the Sun would be represented by a circle around 1.1 metres in diameter. How far away would it be? You may have 10 metres either way.

   c.   Finally, using the same scale, the nearest star, Proxima Centauri is around 31 of what unit away from our 1-metre-diameter Sun?

6 What invertebrate garden pest shares its name with a unit of mass used in the obsolete foot-pound-second system, being the mass that is accelerated by one foot per second squared by one pound-force?

Three bonus questions on physiology

a. What term describes glands that secrete into body cavities or ducts, rather than directly into the blood stream?

b. What serous secretion is produced by the parotid glands?

c. The exocrine glands known as the crypts of Lieberkuhn are found in what part of the body?

7 2010 was the year 4343 of the current era in which Asian calendar, 2333 BC being the year of the founding of the ancient kingdom of Gojoseon by Dangun?

Three bonus questions on square numbers

a. The next year that is a perfect square will be 2025, that is, 45 squared. The last year that was a perfect square saw three monarchs on the throne of Great Britain. What year was it?

b. Which year, a perfect square, saw the denunciation of Martin Luther by the Diet of Worms, the death of Magellan and the fall of the Aztec capital to the Spanish?

c. Which year, also a perfect square, saw the deaths of Edgar Allan Poe and Frederic Chopin and the suppression of the Hungarian Uprising?

8 Described ironically by the sitter as 'a remarkable example of modern art', who was presented with a portrait of himself by Graham Sutherland in celebration of his 80th birthday? It was destroyed in 1956 by his wife Clementine.

Three bonus questions on nicknames used by *Private Eye*

  a. 'The Grocer' was *Private Eye*'s nickname for which Prime Minister? He was first given the name in 1962 as a result of his role in the negotiations over EEC food policy.

  b. In the 1960s, a Scottish newspaper wrongly captioned a photo of which Prime Minister as 'Baillie Vass', having mistaken him for a Scottish magistrate, leading *Private Eye* to adopt this as his nickname?

  c. Born Jan Ludvik Hoch, which publisher and former Labour MP was referred to by *Private Eye* as both 'Cap'n Bob' and 'the Bouncing Czech'?

9 Situated at the point where the Allegheny and Monongahela rivers join to form the Ohio, which city of Western Pennsylvania is nicknamed 'the City of Bridges' and 'the Steel City'? It is named after the eighteenth-century statesman who led Britain during the Seven Years' War.

Three bonus questions on roads

  a. Following the Great North Road for much of its route, and passing through or near Peterborough, Darlington and Berwick, which is the longest numbered road in Great Britain?

  b. The A1 on the Isle of Man connects the capital Douglas with which town on the west coast, the home of the island's Anglican cathedral and connected to St Patrick's Isle by a causeway?

  c. The A1 in Northern Ireland runs from Belfast to the border with the Republic of Ireland, south of which city, straddling County Down and County Armagh at the head of Carlingford Lough?

(10) Listen carefully and answer as soon as you buzz. Five European countries have internet codes that begin with a different letter from that which begins their one-word English name. One is Serbia (.rs); name three of the others.

Three bonus questions on the year 1711

a. John Shore, Sergeant Trumpeter to the Court, is generally credited with the invention of what two-pronged steel instrument in 1711?

b. 'A little learning is a dangerous thing; / Drink deep, or taste not the Pierian spring.' This couplet appears in which work by Alexander Pope, first published in 1711?

c. Born in Edinburgh in 1711, which philosopher's works include *A Treatise of Human Nature* and *Dialogues Concerning Natural Religion*?

(11) Listen carefully and answer as soon as you buzz. Which prime number may be obtained by adding the number of sovereign states in South America to the number of countries whose English names end in '-stan'?

Three bonus questions on an island group

a. Yell and Unst are among the islands of which group on a similar latitude to Anchorage and St Petersburg?

b. Meaning roughly 'End of the holiday', what name is given to the festival held in Lerwick every January, beginning with a torch-lit procession and culminating in the burning of a full-size replica Viking longship?

c. Prior to 1469, Shetland and Orkney belonged to which country, whose king pledged them as a dowry for his daughter on her marriage to King James the Third of Scotland?

12 Quote: 'When a man is tired of London, he is tired of life; for there is in London all that life can afford.' These are the words of which literary figure, in a discussion of 20 September 1777?

Three bonus questions on Canada

a. Extending northward above the Arctic Circle to the Beaufort Sea, which territory has Whitehorse as its capital and contains Canada's highest mountain, Mount Logan?

b. Edmonton and Calgary are the major cities in which province, lying between British Columbia and Saskatchewan?

c. Four Canadian provinces and territories border on Hudson Bay; Nunavut, Ontario and Quebec are three, what is the fourth?

13 Often described as the largest tank battle in history, Operation Citadel, in the summer of 1943, was a German offensive in the vicinity of which Russian city? It resulted in a Soviet victory.

Three bonus questions on anagrams of the word 'omen'

a. 'Nemo me impune lacessit' is a latin motto principally associated with which flowering plant?

b. 'Meno' is a Socratic dialogue that attempts to define what general ethical concept, known in Greek as 'arete'?

c. Nome, a town situated on an inlet of the Bering Sea, was formally the largest settlement of which US state?

14 Examples being aphids and cicadas, what term denotes the taxonomic order of true bugs whose mouthparts have evolved into a proboscis used for sucking? The name of the order derives ultimately from Greek words meaning 'half' and 'wing'?

Three bonus questions on Greek prefixes

a. What prefix, derived from the Greek for 'stranger', forms part of one word meaning a fragment of rock incorporated in magma, and another meaning a dislike of foreigners?

b. The prefix 'xyl-' denotes objects or substances derived from what material?

c. What is the literal meaning of the prefix 'xero-', found in words such as xerocopy and xerophyte?

15 Answer as soon as you buzz. If two bananas and one apricot cost 70 pence, and one banana and two apricots cost 80 pence, how much does one banana and one apricot cost?

Three bonus questions on linear algebra

a. In a vector space, what name is given to the minimal size of a set of spanning vectors?

b. What is the dimension of the set of complex numbers, when regarded as a vector space over the real numbers?

c. What is the dimension of the set of complex numbers, when regarded as a vector space over the complex numbers?

16 Name the two countries whose representatives gave their names to the Kellogg-Briand Pact of 1928, also known as the 'Treaty for the Renunciation of War as an Instrument of National Policy'?

Three bonus questions on physical equations

a. The orbital period of a planet depends on its semi-major axis raised to what power?

b. At long range, the field of an electric quadrupole depends on distance to what power?

c. And the radiated energy of a black body is proportional to temperature raised to what power?

17 Give the names of all three of the metallic elements which have alphabetically successive one-letter symbols.

Three bonus questions on measuring instruments

a. Especially useful at airports, a ceilometer uses an intense beam of light to measure the height of what?

b. A bourdon gauge is widely used for measuring the pressure of liquids and gases and is therefore a type of which instrument, deriving its name in part from the Greek for 'thin'?

c. Used in assessing astigmatism, a keratometer tests the degree of abnormal curvature of which part of the eye?

18 From the Greek meaning 'pure', what name was given to the Christian sect which flourished in Southern France from the eleventh century? It adopted the Manichean doctrine of the duality of good and evil, and resulted in a crusade in 1209 led by Simon de Montfort the Elder.

Three bonus questions on escapes by boat

a. Helped by the family of her gaolers, which royal figure escaped by boat from Lochleven Castle in May 1568?

b. In June 1746, Flora Macdonald helped Charles Edward Stuart escape to Skye from which island, situated between North and South Uist?

c. In autumn 1943, citizens of which Nazi-occupied country achieved the clandestine evacuation of more than 7,000 Jews by boat to a neutral country?

19 What alternative name for glucose derives from the fact that it causes the plane of a ray of polarised light to rotate to the right?

Three bonus questions on twenty-first-century works of non-fiction

a. In the 2009 book *Sum*, how many 'Tales from the Afterlives' are told by the US neuroscientist David Eagleman?

b. Which British professor of psychology is the author of *The Luck Factor*, *Quirkology* and *59 Seconds*?

c. In his 2009 book *Catching Fire*, the British primatologist Richard Wrangham argues that human evolution was driven by the invention of what?

20 A plaque in Medford, Massachusetts marks the site of the composition in the 1850s of which pervasive seasonal song by James Lord Pierpont? Originally written for Thanksgiving, it was inspired by the town's popular sleigh races.

Three bonus questions on Shakespeare's twins

a. What is the name of Viola's twin brother in Shakespeare's *Twelfth Night*, whom she believes to be dead at the start of the play?

b. Which of Shakespeare's plays features two pairs of identical twins, Antipholus and Dromio of Syracuse, and Antipholus and Dromio of Ephesus?

c. Shakespeare himself had twin children. The girl was named Judith; what name was given to the boy, who died at the age of 11?

21 '[His] success was built firmly on the idea that ... you should not give consumers what they want, because they don't know what they want.' These words of the philosopher Julian Baggini refer to which US entrepreneur, who died in October 2011?

Three bonus questions on psychology

a. Which American university gives its name to a notorious experiment of 1971 in which a simulated prison was set up in the basement of the psychology department and students were randomly assigned the roles of inmates and guards?

b. Which Midwestern state university gives its name to a 1944 'starvation experiment' in which conscientious objectors were subjected to malnutrition and their physical and psychological responses monitored?

c. Which US psychologist gives his name to an 'obedience to authority' study, in which people apparently showed themselves willing to administer electric shocks to other experimental subjects?

22 Covering his life from his birth in Oxford during the Second World War to his theories on black holes and the formation of the universe, a recorded speech entitled 'A Brief History of Mine' marked the 70th birthday of which scientist in January 2012?

Three bonus questions on punning book titles

a. *The Ode Less Travelled*, a book about poetry by Stephen Fry published in 2005, derives its title from two lines in a poem by which writer?

b. According to the title of the book of popular science by Marcus Chown published in 2009, *We Need to Talk about...* which nineteenth-century physicist'?

c. Which letter of the alphabet constitutes the only difference between the titles of a 1967 book of popular anthropology and a 2006 book about the theory of comedy?

23 The poet Dante and the theologian Thomas Aquinas were both born during the reign of which English monarch?

Three bonus questions on women's writing

a. Published in 1993, *Oleander, Jacaranda: A Childhood Perceived* is a memoir by which British Booker Prize winner and recalls her early years in Egypt, her birthplace in 1933?

b. Thought to be largely autobiographical, which 1956 novel begins with the words, '"Take my camel, dear,"' said my Aunt Dot, as she climbed down from this animal on her return from High Mass'?

c. Which 1955 novel is being read 'in Tehran' in the title of a 2004 memoir by Azar Nafisi, an Iranian professor of literature?

24 What given name links Valento in the Raymond Chandler novel *Farewell My Lovely*, Von Tussle in the film *Hairspray*, Kelly in the musical *Chicago*, and Dinkley in the television series *Scooby-Doo*?

Three bonus questions on the films of Billy Wilder. In each case, identify the film from the description.

a. A 1950 film named after a major thoroughfare in Los Angeles, it stars Gloria Swanson as a faded silent movie star?

b.   An Oscar-winning film of 1960 in which C.C. Baxter, played by Jack Lemmon, lends his flat to his company superiors for extramarital liaisons? Lemmon is seen using a tennis racket to strain spaghetti.

c.   A 1959 film starring Jack Lemmon and Tony Curtis as two musicians forced to go on the run after supposedly witnessing the St Valentine's Day Massacre of 1929?

25 Spencer Gore in 1877 and Maud Watson in 1884 were respectively the first winners of the men's and ladies' titles in which sporting championship?

Three bonus questions on sporting venues

a.   Which area of West London takes its name from the venue of the 1908 Olympics, at which the modern length of the marathon was fixed at 26 miles 385 yards, in order to bring the finishing line before the royal box?

b.   After a police officer's mount used to control the crowds, the nickname the 'White Horse Final' is often given to the first FA Cup Final played at Wembley, in 1923. Which Lancashire club were the winners?

c.   Which London football stadium shares its name in part with the personal emblem of King Richard the Second?

26 What name is shared by two plants? One is a form of thistle native to the Mediterranean, its edible parts being the bracts around the unopened flower; the other has edible tubers and a name deriving in part from a corruption of the Italian for sunflower.

Three bonus questions on trees

a.   What is the common name for the coniferous tree genus *Abies*, whose species include the Caucasian, Balsam, Red and Noble?

b. Which firs in the genus *Pseudo-tsuga* have distinctive pendulous cones and softer leaves than the *Abies* firs, and are named after a Scottish botanist?

c. Similar in appearance to the firs, which genus of trees has species that include Norway and Sitka?

27 In geomorphology, what term from the Spanish denotes a flat area of silt or sand, usually characterised by salt deposits, that lies at the bottom of a desert basin and is dry except after rain?

Three bonus questions on phases in science

a. What word describes the transition of a substance from a solid phase to a gas phase without passing through a liquid phase?

b. In cell division, which phase of mitosis follows metaphase? It is the stage during which chromatids move towards opposite poles.

c. What phase of the Moon is seen when the ecliptic longitude of the Sun and Moon differ by 180 degrees?

28 Three prizes awarded each year for writing in different media are named after which British author, who aspired to 'make political writing into an art' and who died in 1950? The prize was founded in 1993 by Bernard Crick, and funded in part from the royalties of his biography of the author.

Three bonus questions on England

a. 'England, Your England' is the title of the first part of which long essay by George Orwell, published in 1941, in which he suggested that England is 'a family with the wrong members in control'?

b. *England, Their England*, a novel of 1933 expressing a satirical view of English life and manners from a Scottish perspective, is by which author and journalist?

c. *England, My England* is the title of a collection of short stories including 'Wintry Peacock', 'The Horse Dealer's Daughter' and 'Fanny and Annie', published in 1922 by which novelist?

29 Listed in the Domesday Book, which village in Surrey was the home of the pioneering computer programmer Ada Lovelace from 1835, and is traditionally believed to have been the birthplace in the thirteenth century of the Franciscan friar associated with the principle 'Entities are not to be multiplied beyond necessity'?

Three bonus questions on dancing in fiction

a. What name is supposedly that of an English squire, and is given to a country dance mentioned in Dickens's *A Christmas Carol*, Eliot's *Silas Marner* and Lawrence's *Sons and Lovers*?

b. Named after the French for 'petticoat', which lively dance with varied steps was popular during the Regency period, and is the title of an historical novel by Georgette Heyer?

c. In which novel by Jane Austen does the heroine's mother recount with delight the various dances of a ball, noting that Mr Bingley danced a 'boulanger'?

30 Meaning 'passionate with emotion', what French word links the title of Beethoven's piano sonata number 8 in C minor, and the subtitle of Tchaikovsky's symphony number 6?

Three questions on music and the English Civil War

a. Recorded by Billy Bragg in 1985, which song by Leon Rosselson takes its name from a book by Christopher Hill about the Civil War period, and refers to the state of revolution?

b. Formed in the late 1980s, which band shares its name with a group of Civil War army agitators and pamphleteers who believed in extended suffrage and religious toleration?

c. What name for the full-time professional force formed by the Parliamentarians in 1645 under the command of Sir Thomas Fairfax is also that of a British rock band?

The Answers

1. Zero (a point on the x-axis has coordinates (x,0), whilst a point on the y-axis has coordinates (0,y). Their scalar product is therefore x.0 + 0.y = 0)
   a. (William Henry) Bragg
   b. Ionising (radiation)
   c. Particle theory

2. Kafkaesque
   a. Edward the Fifth
   b. Richard the First
   c. Catherine Parr (Catherine of Aragon also served as regent in similar circumstances but ceased to be Queen in 1533)

3. (Marcel) Proust
   a. *On Chesil Beach*
   b. Great Yarmouth (accept Yarmouth; in the book it is referred to only as Yarmouth)
   c. Jane Austen

4. Aubergine / eggplant
   a. Kerry
   b. Clare
   c. Wexford

5. Japan (the spacecraft Hayabusa's mission to 25143 Itokawa)
   a. 30 centimetres
   b. 118 metres (so accept 108–128 metres)

c. Gigametre / million kilometres (or around 80 times the real distance from the Earth to the Moon; not 'Astronomical Units' – it is ~268 AU from the Sun)

6 Slug

    a. Exocrine

    b. Saliva (accept alpha-amylase)

    c. (Small) Intestines / ileum (allow alimentary canal)

7 Korean calendar

    a. 1936 (44 squared; George V, Edward VIII and George VI, of course)

    b. 1521 (39 squared)

    c. 1849 (43 squared)

8 (Sir Winston) Churchill

    a. (Edward) Heath

    b. (Alec) Douglas-Home

    c. (Robert) Maxwell

9 Pittsburgh (after William Pitt, of course)

    a. A1

    b. Peel

    c. Newry

10 Germany, Croatia, Spain, Switzerland (.de, .hr, .es, .ch)

    a. Tuning fork

    b. 'Essay on Criticism'

    c. (David) Hume

11 19 (12 + 7)

    a. The Shetland Islands

    b. Up Helly Aa

    c. Denmark

12 (Doctor Samuel) Johnson

    a. Yukon
    b. Alberta
    c. Manitoba

13 Kursk
    a. Thistle (Order of the Thistle, numerous Scottish regiments, etc.)
    b. Virtue / excellence / goodness
    c. Alaska

14 Hemiptera
    a. 'Xeno-' (xenolith and xenophobia)
    b. Wood
    c. Dry

15 50 pence ($2a+p = 70$; $a+2p = 80$ therefore $3a+3p = 150$, $a+p = 50$; no need to work a and p out explicitly)
    a. Dimension
    b. Two
    c. One

16 The USA and France (Secretary of State Frank B. Kellogg, Foreign Minister Aristide Briand)
    a. 3/2 (or 1.5)
    b. Minus 4
    c. 4

17 Uranium (u), vanadium (v), tungsten (w) (n, o and p are non-metallic elements)
    a. Cloud bases (accept clouds, correcting it)
    b. Manometer
    c. Cornea

18 Cathars
    a. Mary, Queen of Scots
    b. Benbecula
    c. Denmark (to Sweden)

19 Dextrose
    a. Forty
    b. (Richard) Wiseman
    c. Cooking

20 'Jingle Bells' (copyrighted in 1857)
    a. Sebastian
    b. *The Comedy of Errors*
    c. Hamnet

21 Steve Jobs
    a. Stanford (Leland Stanford Junior University)
    b. Minnesota
    c. (Stanley) Milgram

22 Stephen Hawking
    a. Robert Frost
    b. Kelvin
    c. 'J' (as in *The Naked Ape* and *The Naked Jape* by Desmond Morris and Carr and Greeves respectively)

23 Henry the Third
    a. Penelope Lively
    b. *The Towers of Trebizond* (by Rose Macaulay)
    c. *Lolita* (*Reading* Lolita *in Tehran: A Memoir in Books*)

24 Velma
    a. *Sunset Boulevard*
    b. *The Apartment*
    c. *Some Like It Hot*

25 Wimbledon / All-England (Singles) Tennis Championship
    a. White City
    b. Bolton Wanderers (against West Ham United)
    c. White Hart Lane

㉖ Artichoke (the latter being the Jerusalem artichoke, corr. from *girasole*)
    a. Fir
    b. Douglas firs
    c. Spruce / *Picea*

㉗ Playa
    a. Sublimation
    b. Anaphase
    c. Full

㉘ George Orwell (annually for a book, journalism and blogging)
    a. *The Lion and the Unicorn*
    b. A.G. MacDonell
    c. D.H. Lawrence

㉙ Ockham (at Ockham Park, on her marriage; William of Ockham / Occam; Occam's Razor. Listed in the Domesday book as Bocheham)
    a. Sir Roger de Coverley
    b. Cotillion / Cotillon
    c. *Pride and Prejudice* (the only dance named in Austen's novels)

㉚ Pathétique
    a. 'The World Turned Upside Down'
    b. The Levellers
    c. New Model Army